Praise for
Faith Shift

"I can't count the times people have come to me saying their faith is falling apart and they have nobody safe to go to for help. I wish I could send them all to spend a few days with Kathy Escobar, a wise pastoral presence who understands, accepts, and works with people wherever they are. Short of that, now I can send them to Kathy's powerful, practical, honest, sensitive, and intelligent new book. It's just what so many of us have needed and couldn't find. I'm so glad it's now available."

—BRIAN D. MCLAREN, author, speaker, and activist

"With this immensely practical book, Kathy Escobar serves as both a friend and a guide, offering help and healing to those traveling the frightening road from certainty, through doubt, to faith. *Faith Shift* is a must-read for every doubter, misfit, or dreamer who has ever felt alone in the church. I've been waiting for a book just like this one for years and am so grateful to have finally found it. I simply cannot recommend it enough."

—RACHEL HELD EVANS, author of *Faith Unraveled*
and *A Year of Biblical Womanhood*

"Kathy Escobar is the best and wisest of guides for those who find that their faith simply doesn't fit anymore. She is the real deal—compassionate, truth-telling, prophetic, challenging. This powerful and practical book will bind up the wounds and heal the broken hearts of religion. Kathy is a voice that I listen to closely in my own journey. She is the spiritual director for the disenchanted and the disenfranchised of our time."

—SARAH BESSEY, author of *Jesus Feminist*

"Kathy Escobar eloquently and wisely voices what so many of us have experienced, that the faith we embraced in our early years is a poor companion in our later years. *Faith Shift* helps us take the all-important next step: authentic intimacy with the Divine without surrendering our minds. If your faith needs to shift, read this book!"

—PHILIP GULLEY, author of *Living the Quaker Way* and
If the Church Were Christian

"Reading *Faith Shift* was like being with an understanding friend who gets me. With wisdom and grace, Kathy Escobar affirms the growing tribe of faith shifters who have left church, scarred and unraveled. She makes no attempt to woo strays back into the fold, but instead provides hard-won wisdom for the formerly churched. *Faith Shift* is a life-giving guide for me and my kind."

—PAM HOGEWEIDE, blogger, and author of *Unladylike:
Resisting the Injustice of Inequality in the Church*

"Kathy Escobar is the perfect guide for navigating the disturbed waters of shifting faith. I can't think of a better person to have as a pastor from afar. Her language of faith shift provides a helpful framework for understanding the states and stages that can be so disorienting and disheartening. *Faith Shift* shows the way forward to emerge from the rubble of shaken belief."

—STEVE KNIGHT, co-founder of TransFORM Network

"Kathy Escobar is an explorer of new faith territories. If you're worried that you might be losing your faith and don't know where to go, follow Kathy. She's already been there and back and can save you lots of pain and time."

—JIM HENDERSON, producer of *Where's God When…*
and author of *Jim and Casper Go to Church*

"Thank God for Kathy Escobar! While others wring their hands, point fingers, and theorize, Kathy can be found where she loves to spend her time—in the trenches with those who sincerely struggle. In *Faith Shift*, Kathy offers a powerful resource for those in the throes of their own faith revolution. This users' guide is a true life saver."

—PHYLLIS MATHIS, licensed professional counselor and
co-creator of *Walking Wounded: Hope for Those Hurt
By Church,* an online resource for faith shifters

"For those of us whose faith has been ripped from its moorings by life experience and wrenching questions, we can't go back. As Kathy Escobar points out, we may try—but at great cost to our souls. *Faith Shift* is the surest, wisest, and most compassionate guidebook I've seen for traveling forward into a liberating way of faithful life."

—SCOTT DEWEY, co-director of Street Psalms and co-author
of *Meal from Below: A Five-Course Feast with Jesus*

"In an age when thousands of Christians are experiencing a shift from certainty into spiritual wilderness, Pastor Kathy Escobar brings warm and wise insight to that often confusing and lonely journey. Her astute observations will help faith shifters know they are not alone and that hope, freedom, and renewed passion call from the other side."

—ELLEN HAROUTUNIAN, psychotherapist, spiritual director and
urban pastor, and contributor to *A New Kind of Conversation*

"*Faith Shift* gives the reader needed language to describe the rhythms and processes that many have lived and even more have observed. As the church has shifted, so have her people. Shame is dispelled as deconstruction is explained step by step, and we realize that shifting away from church as we know it does not mean leaving God behind."

—DR. DEBORAH KOEHN LOYD, coach, educator, and author

"One Sunday after I had left the ministry, while caught in the thralls of my own turmoil, I received a phone call from a practical stranger, Kathy Escobar. With great kindness and wisdom, she helped me find my spiritual feet again. Her words helped get me back on the path to wholeness. That pivotal call was this book distilled."

—DAVID HAYWARD, blogger and founder of the Lasting Supper,
an online community for people in spiritual transition

"*Faith Shift* is a masterpiece of permission giving—a crucial handbook for anyone venturing into the unknown of faith deconstruction and reconstruction."

—ANGIE FADEL, licensed spiritual director, co-pastor of
the Bridge, and founder of Agents of Future

"Kathy has the ability to build a sacred space through her words—a place where we feel safe and free to be our most honest self, so we can explore new ways of seeing. *Faith Shift* is a wise resource for anyone who has been disillusioned at the core by the things we hold dear, especially church."

—IDELETTE McVICKER, founder and editor-in-chief
of *SheLovesmagazine.com*

"These are the beautiful stories of the messy, painful, disruption demanded by true growth and transformation—the stories that make us realize we are not alone in this journey, and awaken the soul to the hope, beauty, and glimpses of Shalom that come with the courage to lean into the deeper questions. An excellent book, and must read!"

—PAMELA WILHELMS, president of Wilhelms
Consulting Group

FAITH SHIFT

Finding your way forward when
everything you believe is coming apart

FAITH SHIFT

KATHY ESCOBAR

CONVERGENT

BOOKS

Faith Shift
Published by Convergent Books

Details and names in some anecdotes and stories have been changed to protect the identities of the persons involved.

Trade Paperback ISBN 978-1-60142-543-0
eBook ISBN 978-1-60142-544-7

The poem in chapter 10 based on Ezekiel 37 is reprinted with permission of the author, Cheryl Lawrie, Uniting Church in Australia, www.holdthisspace.org.au.

Cover design by Mark D. Ford

Published in the United States by Convergent Books, an imprint of the Crown Publishing Group, a division of Random House LLC, New York, a Penguin Random House Company.

Convergent Books® and its open book colophon are registered trademarks of Random House LLC.

Library of Congress Cataloging-in-Publication Data
Escobar, Kathy.
    Faith shift : finding your way forward when everything you believe is coming apart / Kathy Escobar.—First Edition.
        pages cm
    Includes bibliographical references.
    ISBN 978-1-60142-543-0—ISBN 978-1-60142-544-7 (electronic) 1. Faith development.
2. Spiritual formation. I. Title.
    BT771.3.E83 2014
    248.8'6—dc23

                                                                2014022406

Printed in the United States of America
2014—First Edition

10 9 8 7 6 5 4 3 2 1

Special Sales
Most Convergent books are available at special quantity discounts when purchased in bulk by corporations, organizations, and special-interest groups. Custom imprinting or excerpting can also be done to fit special needs. For information, please e-mail Special Markets@ConvergentBooks.com or call 1-800-603-7051.

For Jose, Josh, Julia, Jamison, Jonas,
and Jared and the Refuge:
my beautiful family and wild faith community,
you all make me laugh, help me love,
and teach me more than I ever bargained for.

Contents

You're Not Crazy, and You're Not Alone

"I'm not sure what I believe about Jesus anymore, and it scares me." A friend whispered this in a corner of my kitchen while grownups and kids whirled around us, eating and laughing during a weekly potluck at our house. A once deeply dedicated evangelical Christian, Jessica looked at me with watery, pleading eyes, and I knew how much courage it took to say those words. She added, "I'm not sure how much longer I can keep some of these thoughts to myself without feeling crazy."

I whispered back, "The crazy part isn't the questions. It's the guilt and fear we feel for asking them!" Her countenance lightened a little, but I knew the theological doubts she was wrestling with were considered taboo in the circles she traveled.

"I went to my old Bible study last week to see everyone and, honestly, I thought I was going to scream. They all sounded so certain, and what they were talking about didn't make sense to me anymore." Jessica was still whispering. She took a breath. "Then I started to get mad at myself for not thinking through some of these questions before."

We find good things at church that we don't necessarily get anywhere else in our lives: community, consistency, certainty, affiliation, a place to grow in our faith. The satisfaction may last for years, even forever. Like Jessica, though, at some point many of us begin to experience doubts about ideas and traditions we have embraced for years. When those rumblings come, we can feel alone, scared, and confused. I understand those feelings. I've been there too.

In Jessica's pain and sincerity, I heard myself eight years earlier when I started to ask questions. I sensed her concern that maybe even the Refuge, the faith community I co-pastor, might not be safe enough for her doubts. What would that mean for her?

I didn't waste time trying to convince her that everything was going to be okay, even though I knew it would. I didn't try to sell the Refuge as a place that could hold her evolving faith, even though I believed it could. I didn't try to tell her God was far bigger than the boxes we were taught he lived in, even though I wanted to tell her story after story of people who were discovering freedom they had never known before in their faith. The best I could do in that moment was tell her what I always say when someone's faith starts to unravel: "You're not crazy, and you're not alone."

Jessica is part of a growing trend:

- One million churchgoers will leave their church this year, and this number is continuing to rise.[1]
- 23 percent of young adults are leaving church due to significant intellectual doubts about their faith.[2]
- "The fastest-growing religious group in the U.S. is the category of people who say they have no religious affiliation. Sometimes called 'the nones' by social scientists, their numbers have more than doubled since 1990." Current surveys indicate they make up 16 percent of all Americans. (Many of those who have given up on organized religion, however, have not given up on faith.)[3]

These stats are consistent with what has happened in my own life and in the lives of many others I know—maybe even in yours. Lifelong friends who were once devoted to their churches, immersed in Christian spirituality and proud of their faith, have left organized religion. Some no longer want to be associated with Christianity. I know missionaries who are questioning their motives and methods, and former church and ministry leaders who are finding new life in the secular world. Numerous others are still going through the motions of church but know deep inside that something has radically changed in their hearts. And these are just my close friends. Throw in the stories I hear week after week on my blog and in my work as a spiritual director and pastor in Denver, and the list gets much longer.

These people are experiencing a radical shift in their faith. And it's not only in evangelical Christianity, which is the tradition I come from and where most of my experience lies. I hear similar stories from Lutherans, Methodists, Presbyterians, and other mainline denominations, as well as Catholics and Mormons. After years of participating in a comfortable and comforting tradition, countless believers have begun a slow drift or experienced a dramatic event that lands them in a spiritual wilderness.

SYMPTOMS OF A FAITH SHIFT

See if any of these statements describe you:

- I haven't picked up my Bible in a long time and don't have any desire to.
- I don't even know how to articulate where I am spiritually these days.
- I have experienced a significant shift in my theology or faith perspective and find myself feeling disoriented and unsure.

- I have a strong negative reaction to words, phrases, Bible passages, and worship songs that used to bring me comfort and peace.
- I find myself swearing more than I ever have in my life.
- I feel sad, angry, afraid, and lost after a painful church experience.
- I have lost friends and significant relationships because of my shifting faith.
- I secretly worry that God is angry and disappointed with me.
- I feel betrayed or abandoned by God.
- I'm afraid I'm on a spiritual slippery slope and have no idea if I'll survive the landing.
- I sometimes wonder if God exists at all.
- I have lost respect for my pastors and leaders and no longer trust their leadership or authority.
- I feel bored and tired every time I go to church.
- I've stopped going to church altogether because I couldn't take it anymore.
- I feel scared that if I share some of these doubts and concerns out loud, I will be judged, scripturized, or ostracized.
- I feel stifled, limited, and unvalued in my gifts and passions.
- I worry that if I disconnect from church, my kids will miss out on developing their faith, so I keep going for them.
- When I am around Christians, I have no desire to be like them or to be associated with them anymore.
- I see more hope, love, equality, and dignity in the secular world than I do in Christian circles.
- Since leaving church, I feel so much better.

If you relate to some of these, this book is for you. In the pages ahead, we'll wrestle with questions you've probably also asked: What happens when all we once believed begins to become less solid and secure? When we sense that what we've been doing is not what Jesus had in mind for his followers? When we have years of head knowledge but our hearts feel empty and dead? When our tried-and-true methods of connecting with God stop working? When we're disillusioned with church and don't know where to turn? When our faith is shifting and it feels like we're in a free fall?

What happens, in other words, when the certainty is gone and all that remains are questions and doubts?

FALLOUT FROM A FAITH SHIFT

When once-faithful followers begin disturbing the status quo instead of honoring their spiritual evolution, they're often labeled as rebellious, divisive, and even heretical. We attend church less often or leave church altogether. Sometimes we're asked to leave. The anger and guilt can lead us to disconnect from God. Lost and without a map, many of us end up on the fringes of all we once knew—alone, disoriented, and disillusioned.

We become *outsiders*.

That's where this book comes in. I have a deep desire to help people find hope and community in the midst of the wilderness and learn to navigate the sometimes scary process of spiritual shifting and transformation. I'll tell the stories of a diverse group of people who are in the thick of their own faith shifts, share my own messy story, and offer some names and descriptions for the different seasons of the faith shifting process.

This book is not a memoir, a textbook, a "Seven Steps to Finding God Again" treatise, or a self-help book with guaranteed results to squeeze out faith-challenging feelings and put you back into a spiritual box. And rest assured, it's not a covert tool aimed at getting you to "rededicate your life to Jesus." What it provides is an honest, hopeful framework for transformation and a path forward through your own spiritual shift when everything you once believed is coming apart.

If you are skeptical of formulas or easy solutions to complicated issues, good. If you are mistrustful of church leaders, believe me, I understand. (Even though I am a pastor, I am not vested in keeping the wheels of the institution spinning.)

My role in this process is not to provide easy answers (there are none) or give advice (that's always irritating). Rather, I'm here as a facilitator, conversation starter, and storyteller as you navigate your own unique faith shift. Hopefully by the last page you may think of me as a companion from afar.

THE FAITH SHIFT MODEL

Most Christians are taught that faith is defined by an event: salvation. After we "get saved," we turn our energies to keeping faith, growing it, spreading it. But life teaches us the limits of this view. We discover it just isn't big enough to describe our experience as spiritual beings. Our event doesn't cover things like change, evolving beliefs, shuffling of worldviews—to say nothing of disillusionment with Christians, our own painful life stories, and the ever-after promises that begin to feel broken.

The truth is, growth and change are natural parts of our relationship with God. God invites us to be in motion, but often the faith systems we are part of don't. Our changes can feel threatening to those who are used to our believing and behaving a particular way.

A faith shift—what often feels like a failure or an end—can actually be a doorway to something more…something bigger and truer. In fact, this process has been widely studied and named by professors and sociologists.[4] It is most helpfully understood as a series of stages or seasons in our faith.

With a nod to the research of others, I have created a flexible Faith Shift model, based on my observations of the common series of stages faith shifters seem to exhibit over time. I've diagrammed the faith journey stages as an evolving illustration—like something I might draw on a napkin if we were at a coffee shop or a pub together, talking about our changing faith and sharing our stories. Although you may see it somewhat differently or use alternative words or imagery, the point is to give language to our shared but individual experiences and identify the progression of a faith shift.

This book will bring these stages to life in accessible, ordinary language. The outcome you can expect depends on your own experience, but fellow faith shifters have described life beyond an unraveled faith as *authentic, grounded, open, true-to-experience, healing, free.*

I want you to know it's possible to survive a shifting faith and find life, hope, and freedom on the other side. Survival looks different for each of us, but we can indeed find our way. We can lose old beliefs without losing God. We can escape all we have once known and still enjoy a deep faith if we want one. We can shed theologies and emerge with new passion and purpose.

We can find our way forward when everything we believe is coming apart.

Questions for Personal or Group Reflection

1. What prompted you to pick up *Faith Shift*?

2. What three or four words describe your faith right now?

3. Consider the list of statements on pages 3–4 that might describe you. Which do you connect with? What would you add?

4. Do you relate to the idea of becoming an outsider? How have your relationships with your church, family, and friends been affected by your changing faith?

Less Religion, More Freedom

How did I end up here?

—Me, in the middle of many sleepless nights

Every week I get e-mails from blog readers, living either in the United States or abroad, who bravely share their stories with me. Whether long and detailed or short and simple, they all include the same basic themes and stories like this:

> *I used to be deeply involved in my church and committed to my faith. I started to find I believed a little—or a lot—differently from my church friends. When I talked about these changes, people didn't know what to do with me. I've been trying to figure out how to deal with my new questions and old relationships and have felt lost, but also freer. I had no idea there were other people like me struggling with the same thing.*

This week's story was particularly poignant. A middle-aged woman attending a prominent seminary for her master's degree told me, "I am an emotional wreck lately as the ground I have held for staying in the faith is being shaken. While this is a good thing, it is also really emotional. I feel as if all my systematic theology is being systematically dismantled. I think I am probably at the point of losing friends' respect and having my family question my stability. Most of all, I am questioning me!"

The good news is, many of us are in the same boat. Our stories are different but the realities are the same.

I was not raised in a Christian home, but if I attended a church service with a friend and there was an altar call, I always raised my hand, unsure if I was really "in" from the last time. For years I was a seeker, strangely drawn toward Jesus but not sure what it meant to follow him. It was only after I'd been attending a Christian college for a few years that I finally felt something significantly switch in my heart. Then I truly turned my life over to Jesus and began walking a new path. I became a good, contemporary evangelical Christian. Like, really good. I was hungry. I was faithful.

After marrying in my early twenties, my husband, Jose, and I participated in a number of churches in the different places we lived. For a while we thrived. We were happy. We felt fulfilled and energized. We were a stable couple with cute kids and a strong faith. I had no idea then that this comfortable existence wouldn't last.

There was nothing wrong with that early season. We all know people who have lived this kind of happy Christian life for years—or even forever. And it was precisely what I needed at the time. Coming from a broken home with few boundaries, I was desperate for structure, for certainty, for someone to tell me what I could and couldn't do. And the church did exactly that.

Even though I had a master's degree in management and organizational development and several years of solid professional experience in a telecommunications company, I felt uneducated when it came to religion. So I dedicated myself to learning about Jesus—the relevance of his birth, death, and resurrection—how to memorize scriptures, and ways to share my faith with unbelievers. I soaked up as much as I could and started serving more in church—volunteering in the nursery, handing out programs, co-leading home groups with Jose, and leading women's Bible studies by myself. I was busy working for God and loved being with others who looked like me, talked like me, believed like me. It felt purposeful, important, and energizing to belong to something.

Some of you may also remember this season in your faith, when everything was new, interesting, and challenging. If you were raised in the church, it might not have been quite as dynamic, but you know the feeling of belonging that comes from having a church family. Regardless of how we enter the faith, inside the system we learn to conform and sometimes discover what the boundaries are by accidentally pushing against them.

When Jose was stationed in San Diego, we attended a small conservative church near the naval base. I remember asking the pastor about the salvation of people who had never heard the gospel. Without attempting to hide his frustration, he said that the Scriptures were clear: those people would not be saved unless they turned their lives over to Jesus, and I needed to accept that biblical truth. The answer was unsettling, but I did my best to agree with him and move on.

Several months later, I learned how the church viewed women. After my pastor discovered that we military wives were leading a weekly Bible study for new Christians that included both men and women, he pulled me into his office. He told me it that wasn't biblical for us to lead men, but, since I was new to the faith, he felt it was an honest "mistake." I went home and looked up every passage about women in the Bible. I felt my pastor was wrong, and his words made me angry and confused, but I lacked the language and biblical knowledge to argue. I didn't know who else was safe to turn to. The other women in the group didn't seem to care as much, and the group fizzled when there really weren't enough men to lead.

Still, none of these struggles were deal breakers. I pushed down any dissonant feelings and carried on, desperate to belong. I was a master at saying and doing the right things so no one questioned my faith or sincerity.

It's easy to look back and evaluate all the ways I blindly turned myself over to the system and didn't pay attention to the signs. But if you're like me, you know how strong the pull is to be part of God's work in the world through the church. You know how emotionally charged and energizing the early years of faith feel when you belong, fit in, and have a place to learn and grow.

A SAFE PLACE

During my intense season of spiritual development, I received a rare and beautiful gift: a life-changing small group of women who were determined to create a safe and challenging place to honestly share how they really felt about God, relationships, and themselves. They welcomed me in.

Their raw honesty was a refreshing break from other groups I had attended where the relationships stayed at surface level. Here, the women shared openly about struggles in their marriages and families, eating disorders, self-esteem issues, and how past sexual abuse was affecting them today.

As I sat with these brave women, I felt God's presence as never before, urging me to become more candid too. Soon I gained the courage to confess that while I may have looked good as a Christian on the outside, inside I was a mess, filled with extreme shame, loneliness, and a pervasive feeling of never being good enough for God. I talked about a past abortion that I hadn't yet confessed to my husband even though we had two children together. I talked about never feeling forgiven in my heart, even though God's Word told me I was. I finally admitted how alcoholism in my family affected my ability to trust others, and how I often felt that God was disappointed with me because I was always falling short as a Christian wife, mother, and friend.

Through that special group, I learned others were wrestling with many similar fears and insecurities and felt equally afraid to voice them. One of the women admitted how every time she read the Bible, she felt more disconnected from God. She decided she needed to stop reading the Bible completely for a while. Others shared stories of sexual abuse by Christian family members. One young mother began questioning her family's ultra-strict beliefs and traditions. When she brought it up with her father, a pastor, she was immediately chastised and encouraged to leave the group. These women, too, looked strong and capable on the outside and were considered dedicated Christians, but inside they carried deep questions about faith and life that the church we were part of never openly addressed.

PASSION DRAINS

About the time my oldest child started kindergarten, my husband got a new job and we moved to the mountains of Colorado. After we arrived in Denver, we immediately joined a lovely, small, independent church where we hoped to find friends. We were the kind of people who showed up at a new church one Sunday and volunteered for them the next week. But when I entered this community, something was profoundly different inside my soul. If you've ever been a part of a deeply connected, vulnerable group, you know that once you taste honesty, it's hard to go back to pretending. I soon began advocating for deeper relational authenticity—for something better than surface conversations and relationships—in our new church. But I kept coming up dry. They wanted to talk about the Bible and our prayer lives, not our flesh-and-blood stories. They wanted to keep us protected inside the church rather than exposed to the wider non-Christian community.

Thankfully, after I shared my story at a large local women's Bible study, I was able to pull together another group of women also longing for honesty and healing. Again, though, the group was on the fringes of main church programming.

Over the years, while my desire for creating honest places in the church increased, my passion for the larger evangelical system waned. Instead of listening to the pastor's sermon, I made shopping lists and daydreamed about what else we could be doing on Sunday morning. (Please tell me you've done that too!) I started realizing there were no women in leadership—in fact there never had been—and wondered why I hadn't paid attention to that before. Certain Christian words or phrases such as, *"The Lord must be trying to teach you something," "Jesus is in control," "Have you prayed about it?"* or *"You just need to spend more time with Him"* began to make me twitch.

I also recognized a pattern. When I spoke to leaders about real feelings of doubt, confusion, and practical and spiritual struggles in my life, they nodded vaguely…and immediately changed the subject. They mentioned what popular Bible study the church was going to do next or how great Sunday's sermon was. I never got satisfying responses.

You may have been in similar situations. You also asked questions and received blank looks or pat answers. Maybe you expressed a desire or idea for the church and were met with ambivalence or rejection. Or you risked your heart and were honest about struggles in your life, marriage, or ministry leadership, yet faced pithy but meaningless responses instead. Regardless of the scenario, the result tends to be the same: a lonely, empty, confused, awkward feeling.

Because I thought ministry training might broaden my options and legitimize my passions, I did what a lot of leaders do: I enrolled in seminary. After discovering a love of working with people in their struggles with God and themselves, I decided spiritual direction was the right program for me. It had a solid focus on moving spiritual practices from our heads to our hearts and then into actions.

Just as my program was concluding, I was invited to become a care pastor at a local megachurch. My primary responsibilities would be facilitating recovery groups and providing pastoral and spiritual care. Sounds like a perfect fit, right? I thought it was an amazing opportunity to bring my passion for healing into an institution that wanted what I had to offer, so I took the leap into full-time ministry.

It wasn't long, though, before I noticed a host of troubling issues. When our senior pastor was caught having an affair with a staff member, it created deep divides between the elders and senior leadership over control of the church. Big donors threatened to withdraw their support when they disagreed with certain ministry decisions. As the only female pastor, I experienced sexism and inappropriate comments that no one seemed to think twice about. Blatant lies were shared from the platform, excused by the need to maintain order and control. Leaders' marriages crumbled while the wheels of the church kept spinning. Meanwhile, thousands of people continued to flock through the doors every weekend to attend inspiring, polished services that masked what was actually going on behind the curtain.

This is not an isolated incident. In fact, with the rise of Internet communication, we are hearing more stories of misused power in leadership, spiritual (and sexual) abuse at churches and colleges, and messy church splits over theological differences. Have you seen it in your own church? Experienced it through a friend? It's often difficult to know what to do with this kind of dissonance, especially when we're personally invested.

Seminary had not prepared me for this. Still, with a background in organizational development, I figured the dysfunction was fixable with enough attention. Bravely (or naively), I called out some of the unhealthiness in the church. I went to the elders and shared my concerns. I spoke up at ministry team meetings, even though most fellow pastors fell silent because they couldn't afford to lose their jobs. I kept pleading with leadership to consider the poor and marginalized over people with resources and power. I used my voice as never before, knowing I couldn't blindly fall into line like a good soldier anymore.

During these tumultuous months, my husband and I agonized and prayed about what to do with our conflicting emotions. On the one hand, I cared deeply for the innocent men and women in our church who had no idea of the political problems; they were sincerely finding healing and hope there. On the other hand, I was choosing to stay in—and suffer from—a very sick situation.

One day a trusted friend said, "Kathy, this is not normal. They might not be leaving bruises on your skin, but this is emotional abuse. I'm worried for you." Having been an advocate for abused women for years, I was shocked to realize that it hadn't occurred to me that I was stuck in the same pattern in a different kind of relationship. From that point on, something had to change.

Change came, but not in the way I had hoped. After a new lead pastor was abruptly hired, I was asked to resign. I agreed, although I was extremely angry, confused, and ashamed. It felt like a divorce, with the church being granted full custody of the kids. The grief lasted for years.

That's when the shifts I had been experiencing over the previous years rapidly picked up speed, and what began as a slow tilt in my faith turned into a landslide.

THE REFUGE IS BORN

If you've ever found yourself outside of traditional church after many years of faithfully serving it, you know how you start to question everything: *Why am I even a Christian? Do I still really believe in God? Is my whole life of faith a sham? Why have I given myself over to the church for years when it has consistently used me? How could I ever have believed some of the things I have been taught? Am I a blind sheep, following the herd from desperation to belong?* The questions are dizzying.

The best way to describe the feeling is "spiritual vertigo."

When I entered pastoral ministry, God's call had felt so clear. I had given my heart, soul, and family to the church. Now I found myself shaking my fist at God for allowing so much damage to be done in his name. I couldn't read the Bible because I was now frustrated by what felt like its harsh tone. So much of what once seemed certain didn't make sense anymore. Increasingly, I just wasn't able to align myself with old beliefs about salvation, hell, inerrancy of the Bible, and homosexuality. My once innocent and pure trust in church leadership and authority had been transformed into deep suspicion and mistrust.

This was scary territory. How could I as a pastor lead people toward God when I felt further and further removed from him?

Of course, some friends worried. Others listened patiently at first, then became frustrated with my cynicism and doubt. Many wondered what had happened to me, how I had become so bitter and lost. Some began to distance themselves from me, afraid perhaps that I would infect them too. Others warned me about the "slippery slope": that dangerous place of unbelief we're supposedly rolling toward when we begin to see spiritual things in more than black and white. They prayed for me to "come back soon."

Thankfully, though, I began to meet others who were wrestling with similar questions and doubts. Some were personal friends. Others were online friends I met on blogs and through other networks. Yet others were people I barely knew but who had also found themselves on the fringes of traditional church. Many of them had served in church leadership too. It was wild how some of the most dedicated people you'd ever meet could end up feeling consumed with uncertainty and confusion.

Soon, these fellow strugglers started coming over for dinner at our house and we'd stay up late sharing about what we no longer believed or how disoriented we felt. Together we found amazing freedom in the honesty, but also great fear. Were our souls in danger? Were we falling toward spiritual destruction? What did this mean for our families? Even though my husband's shift looked different from mine, we were fairly aligned in our timing, and worry for our children's faith was a deep concern for both of us.

When you come from a faith that is built on standing firm on certain specific beliefs, it's incredibly hard to feel secure when your foundation turns to sand.

The more I engaged with others, the more I recognized a phenomenon that was much bigger than only my experience. I discovered more people were leaving organized religion because they could no longer reconcile what was going on in their hearts with the systems they had given themselves to for years. I met once-faithful men and women who shared stories with similar themes. After many years of being part of churches as leaders, pastors, and faithful attenders, they had experienced some kind of painful, personal spiritual change that left them feeling untethered. Many had gone to their church leaders or risked being honest in small groups only to be chastised, confronted, Bible-versed, and even shunned. Some were able to slip away quietly and were never even missed. Others were still hiding out in their churches, going through the motions because they didn't know what else to do. Often our conversations were filled with tears, shame, and doubt.

Looking back, I realize that we strugglers shared common experiences:

1. A background in a faith system with very clear rules and expectations for participants
2. A significant shift in our relationship with God and/or the church
3. Uncertainty about whom to trust with our thoughts and emotions
4. Discomfort in once-welcoming communities and groups
5. Fear that maybe *we* are the problem—that we are wrong, sinful, or deceived

To my surprise, in the middle of our common experiences, something new was being born as some of our old hopes died. We were starting another church.

You see, despite my theological doubts, I still maintained a wild dream for "what could be" when it came to community. I wanted to be part of creating a safe place for people to talk about faith issues and the damage we'd suffered in our church homes. I was still passionate about social justice, equality, and a place where outsiders, the hurting, and the marginalized could find hope and healing with others. I wanted a place where people who had lost dreams could gather courage to create new ones. I still wanted to follow Jesus even though I knew it would probably look completely different from what it had before. Put all that together, and it seemed that the best way to find such a community was to create one.

Fortunately, I had a friend who felt the same way. Karl Wheeler, a teammate from the megachurch, had lost his job at the same time and for most of the same reasons I did. A once-ultraconservative religious person, Karl had been involved in ministry for thirty years prior to our working together for the last six months I was on staff.

Along with a team of several other men and women, Karl and I planted the Refuge, a mission center and Christian community in North Denver dedicated to helping hurting and hungry people find faith, hope, and dignity alongside each other. Today, the Refuge is an eclectic mix of rich and poor, under- and overeducated, hurting and thriving, young and old, gay and straight, politically and theologically conservative and liberal. We are known as a place where people can wrestle with hard realities about life and faith. For many, we are a church where people come to heal from church.

SO MUCH FAITH, SO MANY SHIFTERS

Hundreds I've heard from or talked with have not been so fortunate. They look for years without finding their own refuge. You might be one of those people. Perhaps that is why you picked up this book, hoping you can feel less alone on your journey.

All things considered, you have to wonder why it can be so hard to find communities of faith shifters. After all, faith shifting is not a new phenomenon. The Christian mystics and desert mothers and fathers knew that seeking something deeper was a natural part of spiritual growth. They weren't afraid of questions and doubts. In fact, they embraced them and trusted the guiding, faithful work of the Holy

Spirit to keep showing sojourners the way. Author and Franciscan priest Richard Rohr writes,

> All great spirituality teaches about letting go of what you don't need and who you are not.... Then, when you can get little enough, naked enough, and poor enough, you'll find that the little place where you *really are* is ironically more than enough and is all that you need. At that place, you will have nothing to prove to anybody and nothing to protect from other people.
>
> That place is called...freedom. It's the freedom of the children of God.[1]

Much of modern Christianity, however, has been firmly built upon different versions of "absolute truth" and conformity of beliefs. This leaves us with three primary options when our faith changes: suck it up and go back to what was familiar, sever our ties with God and/or church completely, or move forward in real honesty and discover a new, authentic faith.

If you are grappling with your faith, you are among the spiritual refugees, church burnouts, and freedom seekers I meet every day.

- *Spiritual refugees* are men and women of all ages and backgrounds whose beliefs have shifted, whose certainty is lost, and whose faith expression is now displaced.
- *Church burnouts* are people who may have given their lives to congregations, ministries, or theological perspectives, but their passion has waned.
- *Freedom seekers* are tired of feeling stuck and caged by the systems they have lived in. They long for more.

Do you see yourself in one or more of these groups? I find myself in all three. I want less religion in my life and more justice, mercy, purpose, and love. I want to feel connected to God, to others, and to the deep places in my soul and not to doctrinal statements or weekly programs. I want to use my gifts without needing to ask permission. I want to feel more alive. I want to feel freer.

Years ago I heard a wise leader say, "The way out is back through." To move forward through a faith shift, we need to revisit the past and embrace where we've been so we can better understand how we ended up here in the first place. We'll start by going back to the early years, where our faith first was formed and our stories began.

Questions for Personal or Group Reflection

1. What did this chapter stir up in you? What are some feelings that emerged as you were reading? Be as honest as you can.

2. Read the list of five things that spiritual shifters tend to have in common on page 19. Which of these are part of your experience?

3. Consider your own faith story and how you ended up here, reading this book. What were some of the significant events that contributed to your shift?

4. Do you feel like a spiritual refugee, a church burnout, and/or a freedom seeker? Why?

3

Saved into Certainty

The Stage of Fusing

*It was so much easier when things
were black and white.*

—JOANNE, reflecting on life in church before her faith shift

"I excelled at church," says Avery, a former stay-at-home mom who climbed the corporate ladder to become a high-level executive after her kids were raised. "'I don't look good in gray' was one of my favorite mantras as I thrived in the black-and-white, right-or-wrong, in-or-out culture of an extremely conservative Christian family in the South. From age seven I attended a summer camp every single year until I graduated from high school. It was one of the most formative and happy times in my entire faith. I loved the safe, homogeneous, Spirit-filled, structured, verse-memorizing, and encouraging environment. The daily devotions, Bible studies, and challenge to live a godly life were motivating. I not only wanted to please my parents but Jesus, too, and worked hard to be the best Christian I could possibly be. Honestly, it came easy for me because I sincerely loved the people, the programs, and the simplicity of that time in my life."

I definitely relate to Avery. Whether it was healthy or unhealthy, intense or casual, messy or simple, we all experience a formative season in our faith journey that sets the stage for everything that comes afterward. Fusing, the first phase in the faith formation (and faith shift) process, is what most religious converts go through regardless of their denomination or faith tradition. Protestant, Catholic, Mainline, Evangelical, Mormon, or other—we all experience a time where we accept a belief, learn about doctrine, and then somehow participate. New faith typically causes an ascent in which we move closer to God by moving farther away from where we were.

Three steps comprise Fusing: *Believing* (the point where we come to faith), *Learning* (where we begin to embrace an influx of theology, spiritual knowledge, and group expectations), and *Doing* (when we start actively serving, volunteering, and participating). Often these responses occur in a rush—all at the same time or very close together. Sometimes it takes awhile for a believer to begin doing what his or her faith teaches.

The three steps build on each other. As when we climb a ladder, the direction we're moving—or should be moving—is toward spiritual maturity (a term that is hard to define because it is extremely subjective and dependent on the church's definition of progress and growth).

Here's a simple drawing of what Fusing looks like:

FUSING

Believing Learning Doing

FUSING VALUES
affiliation
certainty
conformity

Try to recall your own feelings and experiences as you read about this stage. We all come from different places, but remembering where we've been can help us embrace our ever-evolving stories.

Just as we have a family of origin that shapes and forms us, my friend Teresa, a spiritual director and trauma therapist, says we also have a "faith of origin" that is forever a part of our story. And all faith starts with belief.

BEGINNING WITH BELIEF

Believing is the starting point of our faith experience. Each of us has a place in our journey where we came to believe in God and in Jesus. Some of my friends who came from Christian families say they began believing "in utero." Others came to faith apart from their upbringing. Many of us have a specific memory of Sunday school, youth group, an evangelistic rally, or a church service where we prayed the prayer to become a believer. Some took catechism or confirmation classes. Regardless of the method, an initial period in our faith development is *belief,* a specific season where our hearts become open to God. It may have started with a small crack that opened wider over time, or it may have been a full-force spiritual experience that suddenly changed everything.

Feelings in this early stage of Believing fall in a wide range. Those from ultraconservative or charismatic backgrounds might describe how they felt using terms like *humbled, inspired, awed, wooed, overcome by the Spirit,* or *pursued by God,* depending on the type of church or faith tradition they entered. Those from a more mainline Protestant or Catholic tradition seem to describe Believing as a natural, cultural part of their faith experience instead of a specific moment or time period. Conrad, a white-haired widower and retiree with four grandchildren, shared with me that as a Catholic, he was born believing in Jesus and was raised with a rigid set of rules and expectations. Yet, when as a young adult he married his wife, she wanted him to convert to her strain of Christianity and become Pentecostal. Eager to please her, he complied and entered into an entirely new season of belief as a born-again Christian. It changed everything for him.

We all have different stories of and language for what believing meant for us, but our shared experience is that we began by saying "I'm in" or "I choose you, Jesus" or "God is real and I will follow his ways." After we do that, it doesn't take long for us to get drawn into the next stage, which is central to most all organized religion: learning stuff about God.

ADDING FLESH TO THE BONES OF BELIEF

After Believing, we enter *Learning*—the time when we acquire knowledge about God through group Bible studies, personal study, sermons, and church connection. During this period in our faith, we develop clarity about what we believe and why. We examine doctrines and boundaries to learn what is acceptable and what is not. Easily influenced by whoever is teaching us, we are sponges soaking up as much as we can. We adopt the language and common sayings or phrases of our fellow believers.

It seems as though my friends who were raised in the church sometimes didn't experience the same degree of eagerness, since they were immersed in a faith life from the beginning. Still, somewhere along the line, through Sunday school, classes, or ongoing exposure to the church, they picked up the technicalities of faith and learned what they were supposed to believe and do. Regardless of how it happens, our initial Learning phase is a critical part of our faith development.

It's the flesh that's added to the bones of belief. What we learn is what we become.

My Learning years were the most inspiring parts of my faith experience. I was incredibly open and desperate to connect with God by reading my Bible, journaling, praying, and finding spiritual meaning in almost anything. I took detailed notes and shared with others what I had learned on Sunday. Scripture memory was a top priority. (To this day, I still remember many verses that I faithfully and sincerely memorized.)

Samantha, a woman with long brown hair, beautiful hazel eyes, and a quick wit, started to follow Jesus as a teenager. She describes the goal of Learning as intentional movement from a casual believer to a more mature one:

> Ultimately, I was taught that if I was really serious about my
> "walk with God," I would invest lots of time in the process.
> Because I was not raised in church, I was determined to
> redeem the time I felt I had wasted. I felt that, compared
> to others, I was operating from a deficit or handicap, and
> I couldn't get my hands on enough topical Bible studies
> or listen to enough prerecorded sermons. It was as if I had
> arrived late to an intensive course that people had already
> been taking for years. In some ways, I was frantic, as if God
> might all of a sudden give me a pop quiz. I was into any and
> all information related to the Christian life.

I relate to Samantha's story because during my Learning years I absorbed as much knowledge about God as I could. In Learning, we don't learn only theology and doctrine, we also assimilate the rules of the group we've joined. We quickly discover how people in the church behave: What is acceptable behavior and what is not tolerated? What do people here believe and not believe? How do we respond to situations "biblically"? What's okay to think, feel, and do? What's going to get us into trouble?

This type of information is sometimes taught overtly, with leaders stating what is expected. More likely we learn it covertly, gleaning unwritten rules and beliefs that we unconsciously adapt to. Again, Learning isn't only about knowledge. It's also about adapting to the system and becoming good team members who play by the rules. To use a different metaphor, during this stage we're painting in our faith development, learning what colors are okay to use, where the lines are, and how to shade neatly inside them.

HARD AT WORK FOR GOD

While Learning is a time of gaining a lot of knowledge *about* God and permissible behavior, *Doing* is where we begin to act on a lot of things *for* God. It's here that we serve in church and ministries, carrying out God's mission. We hand out programs, sign up to bring food, and volunteer. Excited to be part of something bigger, we work alongside others who care about Jesus too. We attend church or youth group regularly, join in enthusiastically, and feel connected to God and others. Anxious to bring God's love to other areas, we support or participate in local and international missions.

Several adjectives that describe people in the season of Doing are *busy, clear, faithful,* and *sincere.* Our behavior is a central piece of this stage, and we are concerned with not only saying the right things about God and to God, but also doing the right things for God. This time in our faith journey makes us feel connected, purposeful, and needed.

DJ, a former seminarian and pastor who can slide right into any spiritual conversation with ease, was raised in a very conservative Christian home where church was part of everyday life. For DJ, *Doing* meant automatically tithing 10 percent of every paycheck, participating in and eventually leading Bible studies, going on missions trips, faithfully praying for others, and attending seminary. Underneath his serving was a strong feeling of needing to be obedient to God. DJ stayed crazy busy, embracing his perception that "this is what good Christians do." He also really enjoyed it and, like so many of us, felt this season in his faith was extremely fulfilling.

Performance is often a big part of Doing, and the kudos we receive for working hard can add to our motivation. God's love and our actions become inextricably entangled. Another friend, Marco, a rough and tumble Harley-Davidson rider with a deep laugh and a tender heart, went to Bible studies multiple times a week in addition to regular and midweek services because his pastor preached that they needed to be at church whenever the doors were open. He also sang in the choir and spent more time at church than at home. "I discovered that I was really good at performing for God. I felt as though the more the people at church appreciated me, the more God himself liked me, and the feeling kind of fed on itself. I was constantly looking for more approval, more appreciation, and I just kept working harder to earn more love."

I relate to both DJ and Marco, and out of the three phases of Fusing—Believing, Learning, and Doing—I'm still the best at Doing.

SECURITY AND SAFETY IN SAMENESS

Three values or attributes—affiliation, conformity, and certainty— are woven deeply throughout the Fusing process, and they shape us in significant ways. Because we have an innate desire to organize and belong, we align with others who share similar beliefs, are on the right team, and care about the same things we do. Within our group, we speak the same religious language and share a satisfaction of being in this together with those who also "get it."

Affiliation

Jesus's call to the lost and broken drew many of us to him, and we came to faith with a sense of emptiness, loneliness, and a longing to be part of a family. Like me, Chloe felt the strongest pull to the relationships that church offered. An only child from an atheistic home, Chloe felt an incredible desire for family after she lost both of her parents. She was desperate to be wanted, and even more, needed: "To hear that I was now 'adopted' not only by my church but also by a family of millions of other Christians created a huge sense of belonging. I craved the big worship services that fed a feeling of being part of something larger than me, and I loved the knowledge that I was connected to 'brothers and sisters' everywhere."

I also loved being affiliated with a new family of people who were moving in the same direction. It felt comforting to say, "My neighbor is a believer too—isn't that great?" or "I finally found a Christian doctor." As someone who rarely felt protected in my family of origin, I found my early Christian years foundational in cultivating a sense of inclusion within a community—both in the local and global church—that provided deep security and safety.

Conformity

The most common way to deepen our affiliation to a group or cause is to conform to specific ways of being together. Stated or not, every group has norms that guide it. Members naturally adapt to those rules.

Churches or ministries, regardless of denomination, hold overt beliefs that need to be embraced. When Jose and I were part of the conservative church in San Diego, we had to complete an intensive new membership class called The Foundations of Our Faith before we could do a single thing in the church. After we finished, we essentially signed on an imaginary dotted line, agreeing with certain central principles and doctrinal beliefs about God and church. Your process may have been different, but if your heart rate is starting to rise as you're reading this, you know just what I'm talking about!

Looking back, I realize the church offered no room for questioning or disagreeing with the theology behind any of these teachings. Explained to us as "God's truth," these beliefs were ones we were required to accept wholeheartedly. Like sheep, we fell into line, followed our faithful shepherd, and never strayed. Today when I talk to friends who are shifting faith, we are a little freaked out about our willingness to subvert our questions for the sake of belonging. But I can't stress it enough: conformity is a strong motivator for participation in religious groups, and we will do all kinds of crazy things in order to belong. Our desire to connect in this stage often supersedes our gut feelings, and we don't want to be labeled as divisive or immature.

For Liz, a breast-cancer survivor who loves hard rock music and people who live on the streets, fear was the biggest motivator to conform. She was not only terrified of going to hell, but she was also scared of the repercussions from her youth leaders if she fell short of what they expected. She had seen her friends break the rules and end up uninvited and ostracized.

The power of conformity is fascinating. As a consummate people pleaser, I readily morphed into whatever people around me were doing to earn their approval. For example, even though I had a liberal background prior to becoming a born-again Christian, I immediately changed my political affiliation to Republican to be like fellow believers. I tucked my contemporary music into a box and listened only to Christian music. I stopped reading "worldly" or "ungodly" books and began reading those that were acceptable to the group, and I began to wear more modest clothes.

Conformity creates clearly defined groups of who's in and who's out, who's right and who's wrong, who's on God's team and who's clearly playing for the devil. Conformity can give the appearance of safety in an unsafe world.

Certainty

The thread that links affiliation and conformity is certainty. Duncan, a retired military officer turned technology geek with a soft spot for abandoned dogs, was not raised as a Christian. When he turned his life over to Jesus, he went all in—to the point of joining a conservative denomination and becoming a pastor. Certainty was one of the strongest draws: "It felt great to finally have a firm foundation to base my faith and behavior—even my political beliefs—on. It was healing to be able to construct a framework for my entire life on something that felt so absolutely unshakable."

Kristin, a recent divorcée with a heart for abused women, wasn't raised in a religious family, but after a tumultuous childhood, she longed for something clear to grab hold of. Converted by Mormon missionaries, she felt drawn most to their conviction of belief. It was the comfort she needed at the time.

I loved the certainty of my early faith too! My Bible teachers never said, "I'm not sure about this" or "This is just my interpretation" or "I don't really know, but…" They consistently used language like "God says…" or "The Bible says…" or "God's Word tells us…" It wasn't long before I adopted the same concrete language when speaking with non-

Christians. My mother, who never conformed to the principles of evangelical Christianity, often challenged me with the assertion that life wasn't black or white but gray, and I should rethink my newfound sureness. She didn't realize that if I just used the phrase *God says,* it trumped anything she had to say. When she confronted me on my political views, I responded emphatically with "No, Mom, God is clear on what's right and what's wrong [and by the way, that means you're wrong]." We are often indignant in the name of Jesus, feeling tasked to defend God's "truth." You may have your own embarrassing stories of passing on your certainty to others. (My apology years later meant the world to my mom.)

Regardless of how we now feel about certainty, we can't dismiss its usefulness in a forming faith. I admit that I sometimes desperately miss it. In an uncertain world and an unstable family, I felt strengthened by a strong net of absolutes.

Affiliation, conformity, and certainty are intrinsically part of Fusing and help form what I call "My 10 Commandments of a Fused Faith," the unstated and unwritten rules of behavior and belief that guide our thoughts, feelings, and actions as believers. These commandments summarize what directed us during the Fusing process and illustrate what we begin to leave behind as our faith shifts. Each of us has different ones that come from our own unique experience. Here are mine:

My 10 Commandments of a Fused Faith

1. You shall go to church every Sunday.
2. You shall not express any negative emotions.
3. You shall vote Republican.

4. You shall never forget that the Bible is 100 percent accurate, literally true, and perfectly clear.

5. You shall not rock the boat or create division in any way.

6. You shall try really hard to connect with God (and if you don't, you are doing something wrong).

7. You shall volunteer and then volunteer some more. And then volunteer some more.

8. You shall achieve spiritual growth through consistent Bible study and participation in small groups.

9. You shall avoid non-Christian people, places, and things because they will lead you down a bad path.

10. You shall always work hard to earn God's love.

What are yours? As you consider your own fused faith commandments, they might feel comical, angering, painful, or a host of other possibilities. Regardless, it's important to recognize them as part of your story. It might be easy to look back and pass harsh judgment on your commandments—I know it is for me. But I am learning that a more helpful response is to honestly acknowledge the truth of that time in my life as just that. I don't live under those beliefs anymore, but they shaped and guided me for many years.

MAYBE THERE'S MORE

As a spiritual director who has worked with numerous men and women over the years, I'm quite convinced that many of us have been duped into believing our faith life stops with Fusing. Much of the focus includes an us-versus-them mentality. Sometimes we subtly elevate church activities and beliefs over the value of people's souls and deep spiritual development. During the Fusing years, we are often taught to separate ourselves from nonbelievers and "nonspiritual activities." By contrast, I love author Henri Nouwen's wise observation: "The spiritual life does not remove us from the world but leads us deeper into it."[1]

As we awaken to a longing for more than what these first three parts of Fusing provide, we start to feel a rumbling in our souls that we can't ignore. We start to dream about breaking the commandments we tried so hard to keep. We ask questions that we never considered before. Affiliation and conformity stop mattering so much. We wonder if there might be something more to the spiritual life than we've been taught. We begin to burn out and tire of serving the church system. We want our passions or gifts to be valued and used to make the wider world a better place. We find we can no longer ascribe to the black-and-whiteness we embraced in Fusing and begin to see in shades of gray. What made perfect sense starts to feel not so certain. Once-solid ground begins to feel wobbly.

We start to shift.

Questions for Personal or Group Reflection

1. How would you describe or draw the stage of Fusing (Believing, Learning, and Doing)?

2. What feelings were stirred in you as you read this chapter? Did any of your reactions surprise you and if so, how?

3. What did Believing look like for you? What were some of the feelings you experienced during that season of your faith?

4. What were some of the specific beliefs you were taught to embrace during the Learning season of your faith?

5. The attributes of Fusing include affiliation, conformity, and certainty. How do these words reflect your experience?

6. What commandments did you ascribe to during the Fusing stage in your faith? What was expected of you and other church members?

When the Foundation Cracks

The Stage of Shifting

*The solid ground I used to stand on began to
crumble. Everything about faith and church
began to feel shaky and uncertain.*

—MICHAEL

I have the most interesting conversations with people in the most unlikely places. A few years ago I was late to a fund-raising carnival at my
twins' elementary school. As soon as I arrived, I bumped into an ac-
quaintance. We'd never had a real conversation, but she knew I pas-
tored the Refuge and led recovery groups. Suddenly she was telling me
about a global missions conference she had returned from the day before. Her voice was low and shaky as she said, "I was so uncomfortable.
Everything they were saying made me feel anxious and annoyed.
Their focus on the number of souls won for Christ and constant refer-
ences to 'the lost' got under my skin. I kept looking around, wondering if anyone else was struggling with the content, but they were all
nodding and agreeing. Afterward, I was passing out materials at our

booth and began feeling like I was a fake, representing an organization that I'm not sure I even support anymore."

Raised in Christian school and immersed in Christian culture for her entire life, Sarah felt frightened by her doubts and questions. She couldn't share them with her boss, who was also a family member. We talked for over an hour in front of the carnival's cakewalk station, in the midst of kids laughing and loud music stopping and starting. She would only whisper, concerned someone else might hear. I told her she wasn't going to get struck by lightning, that she was in good company with many others who were also experiencing similar feelings.

"Really? I'm not the only one?"

I chuckled as I replied, "I promise, you're most definitely not the only one. But strap in. This is going to be a bumpy ride."

For all kinds of reasons, many of us begin to experience a slow—or sometimes dramatic—shift in how we relate to God and the church. We hit a significant spiritual barrier and things stop working in the ways we are used to. Our connection with God wanes, and we can't seem to pray. Our hearts begin to feel dead. We start to feel resentful. We stop caring about church, and events and programs lose their attraction. We notice inconsistencies in leadership and theology that never occurred to us before. We become ambivalent, apathetic, or feel hints of anger and fear in deep places of our souls.

For some, these feelings come on the heels of a personal crisis, such as a divorce, death, painful church experience, or significant life change. For others, they creep in slowly for no apparent reason. The Barna Group conducts massive research in the area of spirituality and religion. In one of its reports, researchers found that experiences and emotions like the following are the most common reasons for moving away from Christianity:

- "gaining new knowledge or education"
- "feeling disillusioned with church and religion"
- "feeling the church is hypocritical"
- "having negative experiences in churches"
- "being in disagreement with Christianity about specific issues such as homosexuality, abortion or birth control"
- "feeling the church is too authoritarian"
- "wanting to express faith outside of church"
- "searching for a new faith or wanting to experience other religions"[1]

It's a long list, and many of us find ourselves in agreement with one or more of these points. Regardless of how we get there, we start feeling untethered and on shaky ground after once feeling secure.

As I've mentioned, I call this transitional season of our faith *Shifting*. For some, Shifting can be a short transition and before they know it, their beliefs are either coming undone completely or they are finding their way back to church. For others, Shifting might be years in the making.

Whatever shape your shift takes, I define it as the strange transitional phase between the clear boundaries of where we've been and where we might go spiritually. It's an in-between, and we can choose how far we'll take it, either continuing on to the hard work of Unraveling or deciding that at least for now, we'll return to the more solid ground of Fusing. Regardless of where we end up, Shifting can feel scary, confusing, and/or foreign.

Adding to our drawing, this is how I visualize Shifting:

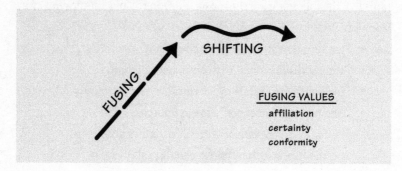

Shifting always comes after Fusing; we can't shift until we have something to shift from. It is the season in our faith journey where things level out instead of ascend, where clear lines become more fuzzy or bumpy. This is where we start to outgrow the values of affiliation, conformity, and certainty.

While people bring many unique experiences to this season, Shifting typically includes:

- beginning to question systems to which we once happily ascribed
- feeling unsettled about particular beliefs and doctrinal tenets
- longing to really feel more known and loved by God and others
- experiencing a deep restlessness that something might be missing in our spiritual lives
- wanting to use our passions and gifts but feeling unempowered
- worrying about losing our security and stability if we lean into these scary and unfamiliar feelings
- fearing that we are doing something wrong spiritually

INTO UNFAMILIAR TERRAIN

My mother-in-law is an outspoken wife and mother who emigrated from El Salvador when my husband was four years old. She loves Jesus and is one of countless Christians who are perfectly comfortable remaining in traditional church systems and value Fusing for their entire lives. They feel a part of their churches, the rules and expectations are clear, and they don't sense any compelling reason to change.

I never want to minimize or dismiss another person's satisfaction and connection. While it's easy for me to judge those who stay in the first stage of faith indefinitely, I am also strangely jealous. I miss the days when faith wasn't quite as complicated, where the rules were clearer, and the ground underneath me was more stable.

Yet, once this strange season of Shifting in our faith journey takes hold, it's not valued in many church systems. Usually questions, doubts, and rumblings about change get in the way of the practical work of the church. Because Shifting feels messy, uncomfortable, and hard to manage, many church leaders subtly or directly create a culture that doesn't allow for it.

Nathan, a father of four with a love for sports and social justice, worked in college ministry for years before he started to shift. He had a hunch that leadership would not appreciate the changes he was experiencing, but he tested the water. The staff member he worked for listened and said he understood, but it wasn't long before Nathan was uninvited to certain meetings and found himself on the fringes. To leadership, his faith questions called his ministry work into doubt.

Before actually hitting a crisis point, my own faith shift was in motion for many years. I felt restless and longed for more fulfilling connection with God and others. I also suspected I could step into leading various ministries in the churches I attended, but I knew the idea clashed with the prevailing theology on women in leadership. I had developed serious doubts about salvation and hell, concerned that I had ascribed to a theology that consigned billions of God's creation to eternal damnation. But I had never heard anyone asking the same questions. While I knew there was a strange disconnect between what I felt in my heart and what I was doing as an active churchgoer, I did what a lot of us do when we start to shift: push down the freaky, unfamiliar feelings and keep on trucking.

When we are honest, most of us realize we experience uncomfortable feelings about God and church at some point, or at many points, in our faith journey. Unfortunately, because there are few safe places to talk about the churning inside our souls, we squash it or pretend it doesn't matter. Worse, we believe—or are told—these feelings are somehow sinful, something we need to repent of. We wonder if we prayed more, believed better, or tried harder, these doubts and questions would dissipate. The powerful forces of affiliation, conformity, and certainty in Fusing can cause us to stop listening to our souls. Our natural instinct is to ignore our real feelings for the sake of belonging.

Jack, once filled with enthusiasm for church planting, began to have serious theological questions while in seminary. For him, the professors' teachings about evangelism and salvation felt contradictory to Jesus's ways of love, dignity, and mercy. Jack challenged the status quo a few times, but he was immediately labeled as failing to believe God's truth properly. He was exhorted to seek the Scriptures in order to reach the professors' and other students' same conclusions. Jack couldn't ignore the fact that in his gut he didn't agree with them. But he also didn't quite know how to navigate the conversation when he was the only one on a different page. He was Shifting, but no one around him was.

Like me, Jack was in his forties. I've noticed that many in this age demographic have a harder time bucking the system than younger people. In fact, Millennials and Generation Xers are entering into dramatic faith shifts more honestly and openly than Boomers. Despite a wave of young people being drawn to conservative faith systems like Neo-Calvinism, with a strong focus on obedience to God's Word, far more are rejecting the black-and-whiteness of Fusing in traditional systems. They are more willing to walk bravely toward the gray and refuse to tolerate some of the injustices that previous generations have allowed. The issues of homosexuality and same-sex marriage are causing a groundswell of faith shifts throughout evangelicalism, calling many young people to exit their faith of origin to stand on the side of marriage equality, among other things.

Leslie, a savvy young woman with a master's degree and dynamic leadership skills, started to recognize how few opportunities existed for women to lead in ministries. She was raised in a church where she could lead children and other women, but that was where it ended. With a contagious passion for justice and community development, Leslie felt stifled and began to ask questions. Her initial small shifts led to bigger ones, and she rapidly found herself on the other side of all she once knew.

My friend Rachel Held Evans, a popular blogger and author, says, "Whether it's over the denial of evolutionary science, continued opposition to gender equality in the church, an unhealthy alliance between religion and politics or the obsession with opposing gay marriage, evangelicalism is losing a generation to the culture wars."[2] These young people want to follow Jesus but not be part of the systems they came from.

Rachel's words resonate with those of David Kinnaman, a strong voice for Millennials and spirituality, who says, "Every generation goes through its own spiritual formation process, but what's different now is that this generation is living in a much more complicated time, and because of that, I think this dropout problem is all the more urgent.... They're rejecting institutional forms of church, but they're not necessarily rejecting spirituality."[3]

SHIFTING'S COMMON INGREDIENTS

Sometimes there is no major catalyst for a faith shift—no painful church experience, wounding from leadership, or specific moment where everything starts to go downhill. A faithful leader for years, Andrew was happy in his role as a church videographer and programming director. He enjoyed being part of small groups and missions. Then he started reading books by Brian McLaren and Jim Wallis that described a more "generous orthodoxy," a different kind of Christian, and that fleshed out a justice-centered faith instead of a me-focused one. These ideas stirred up strange, unfamiliar feelings in Andrew, and he began questioning the insider-versus-outsider attitude in traditional churches and even in some alternative ones.

After traveling to several foreign countries and intersecting with people from different faiths, Andrew, now a new father, says, "I found the religious litmus test of typical Christian salvation seemed not only limiting but also radically egocentric." Andrew's shifts didn't come in a rush, but over a long period of time. The life he had been living made less sense and offered less fulfillment or freedom. Though he kept working in the church, Andrew found his certainty waning and disillusionment seeping in.

A soccer mom with an infectious laugh and the gift of organization, Meg was rolling along in her faith just fine, leading a student ministry and feeling fulfilled in her work. Then her husband began asking significant questions about hell, homosexuality, and biblical interpretation. Issues she had never thought of before started keeping her up at night. When a friend's daughter died suddenly, it radically called into question what she believed about God: Was there only one way to get to God? Where did that leave billions of other people? Was her friend's daughter now burning in hell? Where did that leave Meg? And what about her husband and older kids, who had decided to leave Christianity completely?

Even though Shifting looks unique for everyone, it has a few common ingredients: the beginnings of disengagement from God and/or church, the erosion of certainty, and a desire for a faith that is deeper, wider, and freer.

Disengagement

One day while standing during the designated worship time in church, I was struck by a wayward thought: *What in the world am I doing here?* The lyrics sounded trite and silly. Then during the sermon, the rote, fill-in-the-blanks on an outline while some guy talked seemed like a waste of time. I began to realize how many years I had spent going through these motions. As I looked around and saw everyone else singing loudly and looking engaged, I immediately felt rebellious—as if something must be wrong with me.

Like many other faith shifters, I kept the unsettled feelings to myself for a while. A complication for me was that while I felt annoyed at what was happening at the church service, I loved the honest, transparent small groups I was leading. I also enjoyed being part of the excitement of a growing church and appreciated the stability of knowing my family had a place to go each week. The disparity between my frustration and satisfaction was confusing, so instead of trying to explore my feelings more deeply, I kept plugging along at full speed.

Many people share the experience of a subtle dissatisfaction.

Christopher, a realtor, was raised Catholic. He went to Mass every week for years and tried to maintain his ties with the church. It wasn't all out of duty; he really did like the sacred space and the focus on God. But as he read more stories in the media about the abuse and hypocrisy of church leadership, he found it harder and harder to feel good about being part of the church. Christopher became more disconnected each week until finally he decided to leave completely.

During Shifting, most people maintain some semblance of what they did before things started to change. Going to church, working for ministries, leading groups, and volunteering are usually still part of Shifting. Remember, this is a transitional phase and most of our outward actions look the same; it's our insides that start tumbling during Shifting.

Disengagement can look different for all of us, but the primary issue is that we don't feel as connected to God or alive in our faith anymore. We start to feel flat, and the life that used to pump through our veins becomes sluggish. We rarely feel energized or excited. Our old spiritual tricks stop working.

Meg, an admitted perfectionist who never does anything halfway, tried really hard to stay connected to God during the beginning of her faith shift. She still carved out specific time to "spend with Jesus" and pray. Then she started to notice how hard she was trying and how little she was getting out of it. Scripture seemed tired, journaling felt trite, and as she tried to pray she kept thinking about the words and how silly they probably sounded.

Disengagement from God, church, and/or others is painful because we miss the connection that sustained us for so long. Feelings in Shifting may flood in quickly or flow in slowly, but many shifters describe feeling sad, scared, lost, panicky, disoriented, angry, and hopeless during this time. The good news is that while Shifting involves a lot of uncomfortable feelings, some positive ones also emerge. Sometimes as we start to realize our faith is changing, we can also feel strangely hopeful, freer, more open, and even excited.

Uncertainty

Another attribute of Shifting is the erosion of certainty. Shifters often feel alone because they rarely hear stories in church of others who have similar questions and fears. This is likely because doubt threatens the core of most modern faith systems. Still, the truth is that even giants of the faith world have sincere doubts. Mother Teresa's private letters revealed that during her decades of ministry she had only a few good weeks where she felt deeply connected to Jesus. Most of the time, she experienced an agonizing spiritual dryness.

In a personal letter to Jesus, she wrote:

Where is my Faith?—Even deep down there is nothing but emptiness & darkness.—My God—how painful is this unknown pain... I am told God loves me—and yet the reality of darkness, coldness, and emptiness is so great that nothing touches my soul.[4]

Isn't it a relief to know that someone like Mother Teresa doubted? True, it also feels scary. When I started to doubt in the early stages of Shifting, I heard a loud voice in my head saying, *You must be doing something wrong.* Other shifters hear similar messages:

- Everyone else seems fine, so there must be something wrong with me.
- If I can just pray harder, believe more, or do more, I'll get the good feelings back.
- I expect too much—after all, no church is perfect.

- Who said we were supposed to feel good anyway?
- God must be trying to teach me something and I'm just not getting it.

The noise we hear during Shifting isn't just about what's wrong with us. It can also be about questions we start to ask, theological and leadership disparities we start to observe, or feelings we can't seem to shake:

- Was all of this time spent in church a waste?
- How much can I really question without getting in trouble with other people or even with God?
- Am I the only one who feels this way? Why haven't I heard anyone else talk about this stuff before?
- How many friends will I lose? Will I ever be able to find a spouse if I don't believe certain things?
- Is the Bible really inerrant, without one single mistake?
- What about the other religions of the world? Are all of those people completely wrong, destined for hell?
- Is being gay a sin?
- Why are my atheist and agnostic friends treating me with more kindness and respect than my Christian brothers and sisters do?
- How could a good and loving God endorse a violent church and allow so much evil to continue on the earth?
- Am I going to ruin my kids?
- What will my parents think?
- What if I'm being deceived?
- What will I do for a living if I am no longer in ministry?
- Is Jesus real?
- Why do I feel so afraid of God all the time?

These are just a few, but I'd love to know what you would add to this list. What's rattling in your head about your shifting faith?

Longing

There's something important underneath all of these questions that's easy to miss or dismiss: longing. During Shifting, we can't just suck it up anymore and ignore these questions. We can't make easy peace with the disparities. We can't engage with God with only our heads or keep going through the motions, pretending we agree. We can't make sense out of what we're feeling with the tools we're used to using, and we definitely can't seem to kill off our longing for something more.

In its essence, the transitional stage of Shifting is when we wonder if maybe there is much more to the spiritual life than we've ever been taught, if the wild ways of Jesus are even really possible, or if we could possibly find life outside of going to church. We start dreaming of a place or way we could use our creativity and gifts without being controlled by the church or someone else's leadership. We long to engage in more meaningful relationships instead of superficial ones. We want to spend time hanging out with our neighbors instead of only church people (and without any kind of evangelism agenda). While desires look different for each of us, Shifting is about no longer feeling comfortable in our spiritual skin.

Elisa is a gifted writer and artist who loves studying theology and exploring the Bible. She came from a legalistic church background, but she has always been a bit of a rebel. She decided to study the historical context of the Bible apart from the lessons she was told it conveys.

I began to see patterns unfolding that I hadn't seen before, and I knew there was something more than what I'd been taught.

Faith was way bigger than the rules, regulations, and certainty I was always handed. Themes of redemption and restoration captivated me the most. I began to see redemption through new eyes, and suddenly I realized that maybe we'd been missing the point all along.

This suspicion began to bother Elisa greatly and she could feel her heart stop paying attention at church. She didn't know quite what to do with this longing, but she knew she couldn't ignore it.

Husband and wife leaders Jane and Jim had a strong belief in what the church could be. They wanted to help their religious community to have a greater impact in their city and become more relational and missions focused. Part of this change would require more lay participation from both women and men and less hierarchy and centralized control. The elders perceived these ideas as a challenge to their leadership, which eventually led to a letter to the entire congregation explaining why others should no longer associate with Jane and Jim.

The last thing this couple expected when they expressed their deeper longing was to get kicked out of their church, but this sometimes happens. Many church leaders cannot tolerate change or what they perceive as threats to the status quo. Jane's longing catapulted her and her family into a painful and terrifying faith shift that continues to unfold. When the groups we are in tell us our longings are "bad," it can really mess with our heads.

PRESS ON OR TURN BACK

Stories like these remind me how humanity thrives on easy divides: right or wrong, truth or lies, in or out, good or bad. People like these categories because they keep things clear, defined. We're sometimes told, "You're either for us or against us," and our shifts force us to choose. Hemant Mehta, a popular atheist blogger, says, "Christians aren't leaving the faith because people like us are pulling them away from it. They're leaving the faith because the Church is pushing them away."[5] Not everyone is pushed out during Shifting, but it's one of our deepest fears and a reason why so many of us keep a lid on our real feelings. We're afraid of being found out and what we will lose once others know we aren't as sure as we used to be.

Shifting can go on for years while we consider where we've been and where we might need to go. For some, there will be no turning back. Our only option is to give ourselves over to the even more terrifying and tumultuous stage of Unraveling, where we shed much of what we built in the early stages of our faith. But for others, giving ourselves over to these shifts is too risky. The best way to shortcut these painful feelings is to return to where we feel more comfortable—back to traditional systems and confines of a more defined and clear faith (Fusing).

We can't talk about moving all the way through faith shifts without addressing the realities of Returning.

Questions for Personal or Group Reflection

1. How would you draw or describe Shifting?

2. How do you relate to the idea of beginning to disconnect from God, church, or others? Have you experienced it? What did it look and feel like for you?

3. What are some ways your own certainty has eroded? Are there ideas, habits, or people you are questioning for the first time? What does that feel like for you?

4. Have you seen someone else's faith erode? How? Why?

5. When we shift, we can start to feel a little crazy and wonder if we are the only ones with some of these thoughts. What are some of the honest ideas, feelings, and questions that have begun crossing your mind?

6. Some of the words faith shifters use to describe their feelings are *scared, lost, panicky, disoriented, angry,* and *hopeless;* or *strangely hopeful, freer, open,* and even *excited.* Which of these do you relate to? What other feelings would you add?

5

Turning Back Toward Safety

The Stage of Returning

Something's better than nothing.

—So many people I know

I bumped into an old church friend the other day at a local coffee shop. I knew Clark's family and had worked alongside him on several ministry projects. Excited to see him after a long gap, I quickly realized from our conversation that he was in the midst of a faith shift but wasn't sure what to do with it. He had left the church after some difficult leadership decisions. Lonely, without connection to kindred spirits, he and his wife had been trying to figure out where to go for church for the sake of the kids. He echoed the words I so often hear: "I really want them to be part of a youth group." Then he added, "We church shopped for about a year, trying different communities to see if we might fit again. Nothing felt right, nothing felt comfortable, nothing felt like a place we really wanted to be. Honestly, I was happier when we just skipped church altogether." Clark shared how he was making new connections with his neighbors, something he wasn't able to do when he was heavily steeped in church activities. "Still, it didn't feel right to not be in church, so about six months ago we decided to just go back. It's been okay, and the kids are happy enough so I guess it's worth it for now."

<hr>

I could sense the concern in Clark's voice that he'd never again enjoy the kind of connection we had experienced together at our former church. Nothing is more terrifying than beginning to lose much of what we knew. When my life imploded in 2006 and I was fired from my ministry position, every question I had about church and every crack in my faith began to be exposed. I knew there was no way I could ever go back to where I had come from. My days of traditional church were over.

For some, however, the imploding might not be as strong or the shifts quite so drastic. After a season of an unsettled spirituality or on-again-off-again church attendance and participation, many people end Shifting in a stage that I call *Returning*. It looks like this:

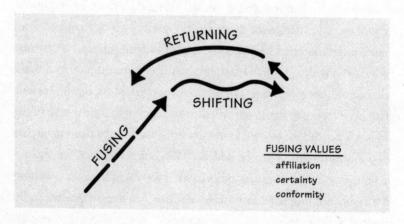

RETURNING

SHIFTING

FUSING

FUSING VALUES
affiliation
certainty
conformity

Returning is going back to the guiding principles of a fused faith, where certainty, affiliation, and conformity are key attributes. For some, it becomes clear that the questions and doubts that got stirred up in Shifting aren't deal breakers, and their souls become more content to remain in traditional church. In fact, after a tumultuous season of Shifting, sometimes Returning can feel like going home, and the need to keep wrestling and questioning naturally dissipates.

For others, Returning doesn't necessarily mean that the low-level angst of Shifting is resolved or that the longings for connection and purpose have magically disappeared. The things that drove them crazy about life in Fusing may still exist. They may not completely ascribe to the beliefs or practices of the faith systems they return to, but they make enough peace with the dissonance and go back to what's most familiar because that's the easiest thing to do.

RATIONALIZING A RETURN

Returning is neither good nor bad; it's real. We need to make our own decisions based on our unique situations. There is nothing wrong with a desire to return or a decision to do so.

Do you see yourself in any of the following reasons to return?

1. What About the Family?

Most Christian parents desire a solid church experience for their kids. We want them to be grounded in morality and to learn to love God and others.

Danielle, a thirty-something homeschooling mom of four, is one of the least likely people you'd expect to leave traditional Christianity. She was raised in the church, attended a conservative Christian college, married a good Christian man, and believed in raising her kids in solid, Bible-based churches for many years. After a combination of church leadership disparities and a serious illness that rocked her relationship with God, Danielle's faith started to drastically shift. Yet she felt as though she couldn't skip church because her husband was still fairly satisfied there and she worried her kids would miss out. She felt torn, but her prevailing thought was that she didn't want her troubles with God to affect her children. So she kept attending every week, doing everything she could to push down the conflicting feelings.

Many other women and men I know experience a similar dilemma with their spouses. Even though they shifted, their partners didn't. What do you do when your mate still enjoys the services, loves the small group, or is in a life-giving leadership position? Asking your spouse to leave with you feels unfair. Often, Returners desperately want to be on the same page as their partners so they find a way to make church work.

Darrell and his wife knew their faith was changing. They tried hopping around to different churches, hoping to quench their thirst by finding a better place. They moved from being evangelicals to being charismatic to becoming Episcopalians. They joined a missionary-focused church, then one focused on worship, then found another small community church. Darrell, an avid bike rider and movie enthusiast, admits, "I would have left the whole thing much sooner, but I needed a place for our kids to learn about God. And the truth was, I loved leading worship and ministries and teaching." Like many of us, he and his wife kept Returning because they didn't want their kids to miss out.

Really, they didn't want to miss out either. We all desire a place where we can nurture our spiritual lives, so sometimes we keep going, even when there's a great disconnect between what we long for and what actually is.

2. Inspiration Addiction

My friend and co-pastor at the Refuge, Karl, coined a term that I dearly love: *inspiration addiction*. Many men and women have an unaddressed addiction to church services or spiritual experiences where they feel wowed. We get hooked on amazing music, powerful preaching, and the hour-long Sunday experience. We come to church seeking a spiritual high that will help us make it through the upcoming week without our having to do anything except sit, listen, and sing. Instead of addressing the realities of what we're really thinking, feeling, and experiencing in the dark places in our souls, we sometimes look for a quick, temporary fix instead.

One of the hardest things for people to give up in a shifting faith is inspiration. Of course, inspiration isn't bad—God's hope and encouragement are important. What's unhealthy is becoming so reliant on it that we will often compromise our values and long-term spiritual maturity to get a fast emotional lift. Many Returners keep going to church after beginning to shift because they are addicted.

I know this feeling well. I was addicted to getting a regular inspirational high every week when I attended church. Since my shift, I am learning to connect with God and my soul in other simple ways that have nothing to do with a weekly worship service. It wasn't easy at first, especially when so many others at the Refuge were also secretly hoping for a burst of manufactured inspiration. After all, they'd left the best show in town, where they knew they'd get excellent teaching, worship, and an injection of inspiration. When we gave them honesty, conversation, and messy community instead, many quickly returned to their former churches or other ones that provided that hit of inspiration. Inspiration addiction is a big reason for ignoring the rumblings of a faith shift and halting further spiritual growth.

Wondering if you might have a strong attachment to inspiration? Here are some questions to help you decide.

- Do you primarily attend church because of the powerful worship and/or teaching?

- Do you often listen to the pastor's sermons online to get another dose of the Sunday message?
- Do you negatively critique church services or experiences that are less than excellent, not funny, or uninteresting?
- Are you constantly telling others about the great message you heard on Sunday that they should listen to?

These habits aren't inherently bad, but they do suggest you might be hooked on inspiration. This will increase the likelihood of a quick return despite rising doubts and questions.

3. Looking for a Spiritual Bypass

In an online class I teach called Walking Wounded: Hope for Those Hurt by Church, I hear stories of people who feel hurt, tired, and disconnected from their hearts in church but still go because they don't know what else to do. Leaving completely is often the last resort. We want to find what's good and hang on to any shred that still sustains us. We want to accept that people aren't perfect and we will never get everything we want. But continually trying to make things work instead of trusting in a new future can circumvent growth and maturity.

My co-teacher, a life coach and therapist named Phyllis Mathis, warns against a "spiritual bypass" in which instead of wrestling with the intense realities of our faith shifts, we unplug from the current pain and quickly plug into another type of church, a different strain of faith, or a popular spiritual program that provides immediate relief. But in the long run, this replacement church prevents us from experiencing the meaningful soul change that a faith shift will bring.

The desire for a spiritual bypass is common, and I know that my original intention of creating the Refuge was to plug into something as quickly as possible to relieve the hurt of my previous church experience.

I wish it had magically worked! Instead, my list of questions got longer, not shorter. My aversion to the Bible increased, and I began to feel angry when I heard any Christian language that sounded remotely exclusive. I swiftly realized I couldn't escape bringing all my doubts and pain into this new church. It showed up in how allergic I became to singing worship songs, talking about particular Bible verses, or engaging in certain theological conversations that felt pointless. I wanted a spiritual bypass, but it wasn't working. What I originally thought might be a shortcut turned out to be the longer road to something different.

There's no question: we all wish transformation didn't take so long and that there was a clear, step-by-step plan to avoid having to live in the unknown. Often, though, Returners miss a new future because they keep trying to make the past work. Others manage to plug back into church rather seamlessly after a season of Shifting and do just fine.

My caution is that Returning can often be an early form of a spiritual bypass. We may also enter Returning later in the messy Unraveling stage, when we start to feel truly overwhelmed with losing so much and can't stomach the prolonged discomfort (we'll talk about this in the next chapter). Remember, the quickest solution to the uneasiness during Shifting is to seal off the reality of our feelings and find a way to rejoin a team. The unknown—what might be ahead beyond the already-difficult season of Shifting—feels like too much work. When we don't have enough good answers to the questions we face, Returning can seem like the best option.

4. The "But What Abouts"

Because most of the traditional church world lives in the certainty and clarity of Fusing, there's a subtle pull to resolve faith shifts and our growing uncertainty with the same tools we have always used. When we think about our changing beliefs surrounding certain hot topics, often our first response is asking, "But what about…?" Some common "But what abouts" you might have heard are:

- But what about how the Bible says Jesus is the only way to heaven?
- But what about the passages that say homosexuality is wrong or that women should not lead men?
- But what about our friends' warning about the slippery slope or throwing the baby out with the bathwater?
- But what about the fact that the church is made up of imperfect people?
- But what about false prophets and being deceived by the world?

Not everyone is a Pharisee, but a common ground we often share with them is our default toward simple technicalities and black-and-white answers. In the Bible the Pharisees frequently tried to trap Jesus with their "But what abouts," asking,

- But what about healing on the Sabbath? (Luke 6:6–11)
- But what about the woman's sinfulness? (Luke 7:39)
- But what about Jesus's authority to heal? Where did it come from? (Mark 2:6–11)
- But what about eating with sinners and tax collectors? (Mark 2:13–17)
- But what about the sin that caused the man's blindness? (John 9:13–34)

When we get hammered with the same sort of questions during Shifting, our thinking becomes even more muddled as we realize how difficult it is to defend our shifts theologically. This dissonance and our lack of easy answers cause many of us to return.

I'm not proposing we should never explore these questions. After all, the Bible says all kinds of tricky things worth wrestling with. But in the beginning of a faith shift, when we lose some of our solid, Bible-infused answers, we easily doubt ourselves and lose our nerve. It's easier to go back, tuck away these new ideas, and stick with the crowd than to move into the land of even more disturbing questions (where we enter Unraveling, the next stage).

IT'S OKAY TO MOVE BACKWARD;
IT'S OKAY TO MOVE FORWARD

Admittedly it is scary to leave behind the safety of Fusing and adapt a more expansive faith. I can't tell you the number of times I have wanted to go back to my former faith out of fear, have doubted my decision and wondered what my life would be like had I never left. Again, not everyone ends up in bondage after Fusing, but I did. As I began to be more honest in my relationship with God, others, and myself, though, I saw glimpses ahead of greater freedom and passion, and a wilder faith. I knew that if I tried to go back, my soul would die.

A crucial piece of seeing a faith shift all the way through is being willing to travel on new roads, to discover God and ourselves along the way. In many ways, faith shifts are healing pilgrimages, journeys to uncover deep truths. Henri Nouwen calls it moving from the old country to the new country.

> You know that what helped and guided you in the old country
> no longer works, but what else do you have to go by? You are
> being asked to trust that you will find what you need in the new
> country. That requires the death of what has become so precious
> to you: influence, success, yes, even affection and praise.

> Trust is so hard, since you have nothing to fall back on.
> Still, trust is what is essential. The new country is where you
> are called to go, and the only way to go there is naked and
> vulnerable.[1]

How do we trust God when we aren't even sure what we believe anymore? Moving from the old country to the new requires a different kind of trust. Since we can't go back, we can cling to the possibility that something ahead of us is good. It takes incredible courage to move forward into the new country instead of returning to the old. Certainty, conformity, and affiliation are tough to leave behind. We have good friends in the old country with shared experiences and bonds. Our kids don't know anything else. We know the words to the songs and what comes next in the service. We might not agree with everything anymore, but the old country has a magnetic draw that the new country can't compete against: history. Plus, our fears can mount as we wrestle with moving forward or going back. What will God think of us if we go? What will our friends and family think of us? What will others say? These fears are why sometimes people stop Shifting and return instead to the predictability of Fusing.

If you started to shift but somehow returned, it's okay. Each of us needs to follow our own unique path. There is no right or wrong way to do this! If the time comes when your longings resurface and you need to move toward Unraveling, you'll know. If you have been hanging in limbo during Shifting, caught between what was and what could be and are unsure of what's next, maybe it's time to let yourself move past this holding pattern and begin to unravel. And if you're already way past Shifting, way over Returning, and in the thick of Unraveling, you'll appreciate where we're going next.

Questions for Personal or Group Reflection

1. How would you draw or describe Returning?

2. After the initial rumblings of Shifting, many people return to the churches and places they are familiar with because they fear the unknown. Have you returned? Are you considering doing so? Why or why not?

3. What do you think about the idea of a spiritual bypass? How have you hoped for a quick fix or an easy solution to the complicated feelings that are part of Shifting?

4. What are some "But what abouts" that people have asked you or that you are wondering about? What questions are hardest to answer?

5. Henri Nouwen talks about moving from the old country to the new country as part of our healing. What are some things about your church that bring you comfort—things you are afraid you'll miss? (For example: the people, the music, the stability, and so on)

6

When It All Comes Apart

The Stage of Unraveling

*I still believe in God's love, but the box I put his
love into has definitely been ripped to shreds.*

—Leslie

Sitting by a campfire recently, I talked with a dear friend about our
changing faith. Over eight years, I have seen him transition from being
a dedicated youth ministry leader to a professed agnostic. Miguel's
process has been deep and sincere. He wrestled with his questions and
doubts for years, hoping he could make it work, before he finally re-
signed from his volunteer position. He sat in church with his wife and
family even when he didn't want to be there anymore. He kept trying
to resolve his dissonant feelings about God and Jesus. Yet, instead of
bringing him to greater peace, he felt more lost, abandoned, and confused. All he once believed felt like a huge sham. He knew he couldn't
keep participating in anything religious and decided that to maintain
his integrity, he needed to leave Christianity altogether.

Miguel made an important point in our conversation: the outcome of
the Shifting stage is in our control. Sure, the earth beneath us begins

to wobble without our doing, and it's not as if we can manage the disorientation that comes from doubt and changing beliefs. But we have clear choices on what to do in response: we can return to the more familiar ground of Fusing (as we talked about in the last chapter), or we can lean into the shift and keep walking in a new, unfamiliar direction—and enter the stage I call Unraveling.

During Unraveling, all we once held dear is stripped away and the things that have held us together come undone. Here we deconstruct deeply held beliefs, practices, and ways of intersecting with God, others, and even ourselves. For many, it can be painful, terrifying, and unpredictable. Others find it liberating and even exhilarating to be finally free of their former trappings. It's where our faith really comes undone—and from where it can eventually be rebuilt.

While Fusing is a season of ascent—where we move upward toward God—and Shifting is where things level off, Unraveling is unquestionably a downward tumble. I picture it like this:

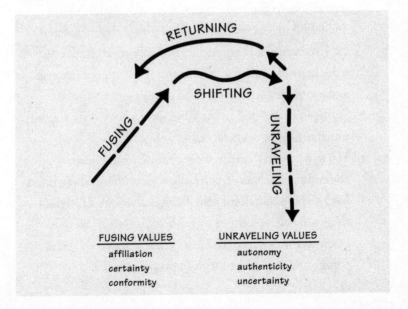

Here's how you can know if you're Unraveling. You may not identify with all of these, but consider the ones you recognize (or others
you might add):

- You have more than a few "I don't knows." Almost anything
  related to faith feels up for grabs, and your initial questions
  and doubts keep leading to many more questions and
  doubts.

- You long to feel some kind of connection to God again, but
  no matter what you do or try, nothing comes.

- Often you wish you could shove all the mess back into a
  box and put the lid on it, but you realize it's too late for that.

- You feel depressed and lonely. Ironically, however, you also
  feel freer and lighter.

- When you try to connect with the Bible again, you sometimes see only its inconsistencies and harsh words.

- Not only do you feel heretical, people have called you that
  (sometimes to your face, sometimes behind your back).

- You feel shame for your changing feelings about God and
  church. In reaction, you either shut down and check out,
  work harder to retain others' approval, or lash out in anger
  and contempt (or sometimes all three).

- Sitting in church feels impossible. When you do go, you feel
  unnerved, edgy, uncomfortable, angry, or sad.

- You may talk trash about your former faith or church
  community, but you actually miss a lot of things about it too.

- Many who know about your changes have cut off relationship with you. It seems they wanted to be with you only
  when you were part of the same team, believed the same
  things, and were tasked with the same cause.

- You stopped caring what people from your former faith system think about you but can't help wondering what God thinks.
- You feel a lot of anger about the past, wondering how everything could actually end up in ruins after all those years of being dedicated to your faith. You usually direct this anger toward yourself, others, and/or God.
- You are open to exploring other faiths or spiritual practices that you would have once considered "ungodly."
- Sometimes you don't have any adequate words to describe what you're feeling.
- You swing between spurts of peace, where you have a deep sense of knowing you'll be okay no matter what, and jags of utter confusion and doubt, where you feel completely lost and sure that you're not just slipping off the slope but headed toward destruction.
- Religious and spiritual songs that used to bring comfort now feel like fingernails on a chalkboard.
- Calling yourself "Christian" feels dishonest. You actually have no idea how to categorize yourself anymore.
- [For those still in a ministry or leadership position] If you're honest about what you're experiencing, you will lose your job or role and credibility in a flash.

Unraveling can be a season of grief and profound loss, where we lose certainty and faith, relationships and familiar structures, and identity and purpose. Our doubts begin to have significant costs, and the losses begin to pile up: friendships, leadership roles, churches, and even a connection with God. Who are we without our tightly held beliefs, ministry roles, and involvement in systems where we knew what to do and who to be? While Shifting is mildly disorienting, Unraveling is downright scary. The lights don't just go dim—they often fade to black altogether. We find ourselves fumbling in the dark, wondering how we ended up here after investing so much heart and passion in building our faith.

In many ways, Unraveling is like a game of spiritual Jenga. Over many years of Fusing we have built a tower of beliefs and practices. During Unraveling, we begin to pull these things out, unsure what it means for the rest of our faith. We wonder, *If I take out this piece, is the whole Christian tower going to fall? Will losing this piece end the game entirely? How far can I go before my whole faith crumbles?* In future chapters we'll talk more about the pieces many of us take out during this deconstruction process, but the bottom line is this: Unraveling is unnerving.

ONE UNRAVELING IS NOT LIKE ANOTHER

Unraveling looks radically different for each of us. There's no right or wrong way.

While I have unraveled in many ways, I have still been part of leading a faith community for the past eight years. Some people who gave up church altogether might question whether mine was a real Unraveling, but I hold to this truth: my Unraveling looks like my Unraveling, and yours will look like yours. We have a lot in common, but our experiences remain profoundly unique. Although I have never completely severed from God (more on that later) and don't know exactly what that feels like, I have walked alongside many men and women who have lost their faith altogether—some for a while, some indefinitely. I have deep compassion for them in that struggle.

We each have our own stories, and as we travel through these next chapters, my hope is that you connect with your own losses and feel what needs to be felt instead of evaluating it against an imaginary measure. Don't look at the person next to you, don't compare yourself to me, don't create an ideal of what Unraveling is supposed to look. Above all, *don't invalidate your story.* What's happening inside your soul is too important to minimize or try to breeze through. Own your beautiful, messy, individual experience and spend time processing what's in your heart and head.

NAMING NEGATIVE FEELINGS

Before I unraveled, any sort of negative feeling like sadness, anger, or fear was something I scorned and prayed against. I saw it as a sure sign that I was not being faithful enough as a Christian. Many faith cultures tell us to strive to be happy and content all the time, and these messages are embedded in our psyche.

Since then, I've found that in our basic human DNA is a tendency to avoid pain and maintain control. Add being part of faith systems that subtly and directly discourage us from sharing our real feelings, and it's even harder. Exposing how we really feel, good and bad, makes us even more uncomfortable. Author and researcher Dr. Brené Brown nails this idea in her book *Daring Greatly:*

> We love seeing raw truth and openness in other people, but we're afraid to let them see it in us.... Vulnerability is the birthplace of love, belonging, joy, courage, empathy, and creativity. It is the source of hope, empathy, accountability, and authenticity. If we want greater clarity in our purpose or deeper and more meaningful spiritual lives, vulnerability is the path.[1]

Unraveling requires vulnerability. It's tough to let ourselves feel painful feelings and speak freely about the crazy stuff going on in our heads and hearts. As a pastor, I find it even harder because there's an expectation that leaders are supposed to be clear and certain when it comes to God stuff. Seminaries don't teach "I don't know" responses. Yet the more I talk honestly with other pastors and ministry leaders, the more I realize how many are silently Unraveling and have no safe places to talk about their experiences.

Although many more feelings are associated with the season of Unraveling, most of them fall into five feelings that are often associated with grief: *sadness, anger, confusion, fear,* and *shame.* The first four are the main ones that I was taught not to feel as a good Christian. Sadness, we hear, is often a sign we're not properly feeling God's joy. Anger means we're not holding a gentle spirit of grace and peace. Confusion is about not being strong enough in our faith. And fear somehow means we're not trusting God properly. Finally, shame reigns over them all. These messages are a significant reason why Unraveling is disorienting. Not all of us feel these emotions in the same way, but most faith shifters seem to relate to them.

Sadness

Sadness results from loss and can sometimes lead to depression. We miss what once was—the connection, purpose, clarity, and sense of belonging.

My friend Avery, who has a Southern lilt and a smile that lights up the room, is married to a pastor. For many years she felt very connected to the Baptist church she was part of. Then her husband got restless and wanted to lead something innovative and more community focused. This new ministry led to another new ministry and another every few years. Avery dutifully went along for the ride but always longed for her original, secure, stable place in their former church. For a while, she went through the motions and tried to play along, but then a profound sadness set in, a realization that despite all of her years serving God and the church, she somehow was left with nothing. Over several decades of following in her husband's footsteps, Avery had lost her network of friends, her passion for singing, and eventually her desire to connect with God. Slowly, she found that all her former spiritual practices and connection had eroded, and all that remained was a dull, gray sadness.

Avery never felt hurt by the church directly, but after her husband lost his last ministry job in a painful split, she disconnected completely from any church community. She had no desire to engage with anything related to the system she had spent so much time serving. The result was that, over time, her once-clear and certain faith ended up ragged in a tangle of unknowns, and depression anchored in her heart.

Anger

Often we find anger underneath sadness. It is a confusing emotion for most of us, especially if we have never had a healthy version modeled to us or were taught not to "let the sun go down while you are still angry" (Ephesians 4:26). We are encouraged to have righteous anger about hot topics such as politics and religion when it aligns with the church's beliefs, but our personal anger is not acceptable. Yet this emotion is a significant piece of Unraveling. We often feel mad at God, at the church, at ourselves, at others.

When I first moved beyond Shifting into a tumultuous Unraveling, I was filled with anger. I felt severely wounded by the church I had given my soul to serve. When I lost my job, I felt as though I was tossed to the curb like a piece of garbage. Prior to this, my typical way of dealing with this kind of pain was to pull myself up by my bootstraps and carry on with a smile on my face. But this time, I knew I needed to process it differently.

So I let myself be angry. Not just a little mad...but incensed. It came out in conversations where instead of pretending everything was "fine" when people asked me how I was, I actually told the truth without editing. I talked out loud in the car, having imaginary arguments with my adversaries—which I always won. I went for long runs by myself and let my feet pound the pavement while I listened to songs like the Dixie Chicks's "Not Ready to Make Nice" (and I don't even like country music). I scribbled furiously in my journal. I took walks with dear friends and rambled the entire route about all the reasons I was mad. It was utterly foreign and incredibly freeing at the same time. I knew that if I didn't express honest feelings, I was going to implode.

About three months into my Unraveling process, a friend asked when I was going to stop being so angry. He was afraid I would become bitter. I completely lost it, crying, "This is the first time in my whole entire life I have allowed myself to feel negative feelings, and I am not going to run away from them! You're going to have to trust my process. I'm not sure where it will lead, but I know if I push these feelings down, I will end up far more bitter and angry in the end."

He was a little taken aback, but over time he's been an amazing companion in Unraveling. We've both realized that bitterness comes when we don't let ourselves feel anger in healthy ways. At the same time, I respect that many of us don't have the fight within us, the right words, or the confidence we are even on the right track. And the first time someone questions our anger, we may feel intense shame. My hope for all of us is that we keep finding ways to let our anger out in safe places. This can happen alone, in a gym, on a hike, in a therapist's or spiritual director's office, in recovery groups, in coffee shops with trusted friends, or with pockets of people you know will not try to shut your negative feelings down.

Confusion

Another feeling during Unraveling is confusion. After many years of feeling certain in our fused faith, we can be completely perplexed at such muddled feelings now. We wonder if all of the confusion exists because we aren't listening to God, or if we are somehow being disobedient and brought this on ourselves. Because those around us seem fine, we question if something is just wrong with us. We feel lost and disoriented.

Even with young children and a supportive wife, DJ actually became suicidal during Unraveling. He had lost his ministry job, couldn't provide for his family, and when he tried to get counseling to process his confusing feelings, he ended up with Christian counselors who kept trying to get him to return to his faith. The atheist counselor he switched to then told DJ to abandon his faith completely, which he wasn't prepared to do. This kind of stuck-between-two-worlds confusion is common and a core feeling during Unraveling.

Fear

Fear is a prevailing feeling for faith shifters because it's troubling to lose all we once held dear. We question if we will ever feel stable ground beneath our feet again, or if we'll really find life on the other side of Unraveling. We wonder, *What is it like not to be part of a church? What if I never feel connected to God again? Without my manual, what codes or values do I live by? What if I'm completely abandoned by God, my friends, and my family? What about my salvation?* For some, it's just mildly scary and unsettling to unravel, while others feel truly terrified because there is so much to lose.

Miguel, the friend mentioned at the opening of this chapter, is one of the most fearless people I know. Yet when it came to his Unraveling, he couldn't manage how afraid he felt. While he had been slowly Shifting for years, once things began to come undone, it happened fast, leaving him and those around him reeling. Because he and his wife had been united in their faith for many years, his deconstruction rocked their security. *Was he leading them down a destructive path? What if he wasn't throwing the baby out with the bathwater, as some people accused, but actually realizing, there is no baby? What was truth if everything he'd banked it on fell apart?* These kinds of questions kept Miguel up at night, and one of the most frightening parts was the realization that he might not ever find a satisfying answer.

Shame

Underneath these four emotions is another powerful and insidious one for many unravelers: shame. Christians are pretty good at talking about guilt, but shame is a far darker force. Brené Brown clarifies the difference between guilt and shame:

> *Guilt = "I did something bad."*
> *Shame = "I am bad."* [2]

Most of us feel heavy guilt during Unraveling as we shed beliefs and practices that used to be important to us and are still important to others. But what often underlies our guilt is a huge heap of shame— pervasive, distressing feelings that we weren't faithful enough, strong enough, good enough, or special enough to hold on to God and/or church in the same way other people could. We feel that something is fundamentally wrong with us, that God might be disgusted with us too. A voice in our head says:

You are weak.

You are being deceived.

If you would just _____, things wouldn't be so hard.

You are not worthy of love, freedom, peace, or joy.

Some of us feel shame for the changes we are experiencing or also begin to reckon with how much shame is embedded in the fabric of our religion. When I go walking with my dear friend Sophia, we talk a lot about shame, especially during faith shifts. She said, "Shame silently drove every aspect of my life. I felt 'less than' in every way, and everything I did was unconsciously motivated by a desire to escape that terrible feeling." Even after over forty years of being a faithful follower of Jesus, and knowing all the right verses about freedom and healing, Sophia felt something essential in her was "flawed, defective, hopeless, and irrevocably broken." The hope of her Christian life for many years was that she could give her "old, yucky, shame-filled existence to Jesus, and in exchange, he would make me everything I ever wanted to be: clean, accepted, whole, righteous, without blame, and somehow superior." This felt like salvation to her for decades—then some of her foundational beliefs about Jesus began to unravel. She was left with this reality: she had built an entire faith system upon a belief that she was inherently bad and needed to be freed from her shame. When that belief unraveled, what was left?

Shame has a way of piling up: shame for living in a shame-based system for so long, shame for feeling shame, and shame for leading others down the same path for so many years. I am oh-too-familiar with it. It reared its head often during my faith shifting and sometimes still tries to rob me of new life on the other side. But like sadness, anger, confusion, and fear, the more I name it, own it, and am honest about it, the less power shame has in my life.

At the Refuge, we have a culture of honesty that is incredibly challenging and healing at the same time. In a recent healthy conflict with my friend and co-pastor, Karl, over some differences in our theology (I have shed some beliefs that he still holds to), a safe space to speak shame out loud was helpful. I was able to say to him, "I feel shame for my changed beliefs, as if maybe I am unfaithful and rebellious in your eyes and less of a Christian." He admitted that he too felt shame for his differing beliefs and has felt afraid to acknowledge and own them for fear of losing our friendship. We both felt relief afterward. Getting shame out on the table instead of keeping it hidden helps loosen its grip.

These are all hard emotions to engage with. But avoiding them won't help. If we trust the process and allow ourselves to feel and move through the feelings, over time we can be transformed and set free.

KEEP GOING

Some have likened the process of Unraveling (and eventually Rebuilding) to giving birth. As a mom of five children, I did learn a thing or two through my birthing experiences that seem to parallel faith shifting. Midwives coached me through three of the deliveries. If I compare my midwife births to the one with a doctor (when I had my only daughter), there is no comparison in terms of the love, care, nurturing, and support that I received. My midwives were gentle, strong, challenging, present, wise, compassionate, and patient in a time of extreme pain.

This metaphor is an important one for those of us experiencing deep spiritual shifts. We need patient guides, people to hold our hands and remind us to breathe, people who recognize and respect the process, and who don't try to rush it or make us numb it out.

When people begin to unravel, many of them hear "You just need to read this," "Stop doing that," "Believe this," or "Work toward that." Consciously or unconsciously, our friends or family have an agenda. They want to get us back on track. They give us books to read and scriptures to reflect on, and they tell us they'll pray for us. Instead of helping us in the midst of our pain by remaining present, many offer quick solutions that reduce their own anxiety and cover up the reality: Unraveling hurts.

There's no way around it. But it's not an endless, bottomless pit of pain. We need people to remind us of this truth. This is why spiritual guides, therapists, safe friends, and fellow sojourners are so important for this journey. Whether online or in real life, their presence is invaluable. Again, if you're not sure where to find them, I've included some ideas in the Other Resources at the end of the book.

Unraveling takes time—usually years, not months—but it has a purpose, even if we can't see it at first. I can't promise a new beautiful baby after one last push, but I do know that the sadness, anger, confusion, fear, and shame don't last forever. We really can come out on the other side in a new place. First we need to acknowledge some elements of the Unraveling process going in:

- Unraveling involves loss. It's not a place where we rebuild or find what works or try to make peace with the past—that comes later. It's where we experience and respect the realities of losing beliefs, practices, relationships, structures, identity, and purpose.

- Resistance makes it worse. We must embrace the feelings as a natural part of our developing faith, letting them heal and restore us. We can't get mad at ourselves or pray for the feelings to go away instead.

- Keep the values of autonomy, authenticity, and uncertainty in front of us. They are key to Unraveling and will help strengthen us during the darkness. Remember that your desire to stand on your own two feet and discover what you really believe is a sign of maturity, not weakness. Practicing honesty and living with raw and scary feelings are part of your growth. Embracing uncertainty as a key ingredient to faith is wise, not reckless.

- We can't know the ending once we've started. In childbirth, we know a baby will be at the end. There's no promise how long our labor will be. In Unraveling, we aren't quite sure what will emerge or how long it will take, and we have to live with that unknown. If we think, *Once I get through this, I'll get my old passion back,* we will be sorely disappointed. The old is definitely gone, new is coming, but we don't yet know what it looks like. This is a tough point to embrace—that our faith experience as we knew it will never be the same. The past is indeed gone and a new future is before us. The good news? Over time our faith can become much stronger and freer than we ever even hoped.

LONGING FOR FREEDOM, DIVERSITY, AND MYSTERY

Underneath the Unraveling process is a compelling desire for something more. The attributes of affiliation, conformity, and certainty we gleaned in Fusing are no longer enough. They don't fulfill or hold our faith together anymore.

After years of conforming, many of us now long for *freedom.* Instead of people pleasing and conforming to be part of the group, we want to find our voice and passion and feel free to lead, grow, learn, experience, practice, and try new things without asking for permission. Many of us are also tired of trying to convince others of anything and want to accept people just as they are (and ourselves too). We want to be free of labels, stereotypes, and being connected with anything that remotely looks like control and exclusivity.

Another value that guides Unraveling is a desire for *diversity*. We're tired of groups of people who all believe the same things. We are done making sure that what we believe, the advice we give, and the conversations we have meet others' criteria of "acceptable." We want to be with people of all shapes, sizes, and beliefs, and learn from each other. We want to live in the tension of our differences instead of squeezing them out or having to choose sides.

Last, instead of certainty in our beliefs about God, we long for *mystery*. We have a hunch God's far bigger than we've ever been taught. We want to have honest conversations about what we don't know instead of what we do. It is strange how dangerous the word "mystery" is for some. It can be the sure sign of the slippery slope, but the truth is that God has always been a mystery. It's the teachings we have followed that have tried to force what's incomprehensible into small, protected boxes.

Like so many of us, when Miguel started Unraveling, he didn't consciously think, *I want more freedom, diversity, and mystery in my life.* Instead, he just knew that everything he had once believed about Jesus and church and being a Christian had come undone. But I believe that a desire for freedom, diversity, and mystery was hibernating underneath, trying to emerge, and that is what propelled him into his free fall.

The only way to get to these three things is to unravel. We can't hold on to everything that brought us security and comfort in Fusing and also move toward freedom, diversity, and mystery. But how can we take good care of our souls while we live in this in-between space? How can we survive losing all we once knew? What might help in the midst of the discomfort and confusion?

Before we uncover the different things we lose in Unraveling, it's important to spend time talking about taking care of our souls during the process. Unraveling is brutal soul work. It involves the deepest part of us—our spirituality—and it's important that we take some good steps to tend to our souls as we deconstruct. That's what we will talk about next.

Questions for Personal or Group Reflection

1. How would you draw or describe this idea of Unraveling?

2. On pages 66–67, review the list of ways you can tell you are Unraveling. Which of these do you relate to? What would you add?

3. Consider the first four of the primary emotions of Unraveling: sadness, anger, confusion, and fear. What does each look and feel like for you right now?

4. On a scale of 1 to 10 (1 being easy and 10 being hard), how difficult is it for you to let yourself feel these feelings? Think

of an adjective for each of the four that describes how you feel about experiencing this emotion. (For example: Sadness: overemotional. Anger: sinful. Confusion: tired.)

5. Shame is a very powerful feeling for many of us during Unraveling. What are some of the shame-infused messages that rattle in your head during this season of a changing faith? (Often these start with *You aren't...*)

6. The desire for freedom, diversity, and mystery is underneath Unraveling, even if we aren't conscious of it. Do you recognize a desire for any of these things? How?

Soul Care for Unravelers

I am tired of talking, tired of processing,
tired of feeling this way.
—Kelly

When I was young in my faith and in the thick of Fusing, I prided myself on needing very little sleep. Even after a full day of taking care of my family, I could stay up late working on the long list of church volunteer projects I had too quickly committed to, and then get up early and go, go, go, again the next day. Years later, when I started doing some personal healing work, I realized that my compulsion to work so hard came from feeling the need to perform for God and others so they would love me. I had always been a helper and achiever in my family of origin, so it meshed with working my tail off in my Christianity—and all the while I completely neglected my body and soul.

As I started getting healthier, I realized how difficult it was to do anything good for myself. Resting, napping, taking a day off, going to the movies, and letting my house be a wreck were all nearly impossible for me at that time. It's very different today.

Many of us come from faith traditions where people commonly

quote the motto "Love God; love your neighbors." The problem is that an important part of this verse has been conveniently lost. The scripture actually says, "Love the Lord your God with all your heart, all your soul, all your mind, and all your strength. The second is equally important: 'Love your neighbor *as yourself.*' No other commandment is greater than these" (Mark 12:30–31, emphasis added).

Many of us were taught that loving ourselves or saying no to others' requests was a sin of self-centeredness. In reality, it is foundational to loving our neighbors properly. Because so many of us have grown up in our faith feeling insecure, unworthy, and unlovable in God's eyes, we love our neighbor from that broken place instead of a secure, free one. It's also why a lot of us are horrible at taking care of ourselves. We've been led to believe that everything in our lives should be about God and others. We've sadly missed the point that our ability to love God and others comes from how we love ourselves.

Still, no matter how passionate I am about raising this banner, caring for my soul and believing I can love myself don't come easily. A nagging voice in my head often tells me it's unnecessary and a waste of time, that I have more important work to do.

During the unpredictable, difficult season of Unraveling, tender loving care of our hearts, bodies, and minds is imperative. Some faith shifters can come through Unraveling relatively unscathed. The process is freeing for them. If that's you, celebrate this gift! At the same time, I know many men and women who became physically sick, deeply depressed, and completely drained during Unraveling because they underestimated how hard all of these changes were going to be. It's easy to dismiss the magnitude of the trauma by thinking something must be wrong with us for struggling. Many Unraveling survivors initially work harder and do just about anything to cover up the pain. A healthy step during faith shifts is to respect early on that we can't just carry on with business as usual when everything we once embraced begins to fall away. We need to adjust our expectations of ourselves, of God, of others.

I relate to Emily, a mother and former leader in her church who finally left after one too many exasperating conversations about women in leadership. A high achiever, Emily thought she could plow her way through a faith shift too. She read every popular blog she could, signed up for our online class, and was sure that she could get herself back onto solid ground in a few months. But as she started to dig a little deeper, she realized there was more grief, more pain from being dismissed for her gender than she'd understood. She started to realize that there was no fast track through Unraveling, and she would have to navigate those waters more slowly and deeply.

There are ways to take care of our souls and things to avoid as we do this deeper spiritual work of transformation and healing. As we look at these ideas together, glean what might be helpful to you. We're all wired differently, and some will make more sense to you than others. During Unraveling we can feel misunderstood, exhausted, desperate, and lost. But we can also gain some strength and hope that will sustain us.

KEEPING YOURSELF TOGETHER WHILE YOU'RE UNRAVELING

Here are several ideas.

Get Used to Blank Stares and Nervous Twitches

People don't know how to react when we start sharing our shifting theological views. The dissonance is confusing for them. We might speak in a raw and unedited way, and that can make others uncomfortable. Their distant responses can make us feel rejected. Remember that many can't get their heads around why we aren't playing the game anymore and they may feel threatened. We have to live with their silence or discomfort and prepare to be misunderstood. Meanwhile, we can also let people who aren't Unraveling maintain their beliefs without criticizing or judging. While we don't understand how they can live with the status quo, we can respect their decision to do so.

Expect the Unexpected

In many ways, Unraveling is a grieving process. Grief comes in waves and can be really slow and unpredictable. Author and grief researcher Hope Edelman says, "It's not linear. It's not predictable. It's anything but smooth and self-contained. Someone did us a grave injustice by first implying that mourning has a distinct beginning, middle, and end. That's the stuff of short fiction. It's not real life."[1] Accepting grief as part of a changing faith instead of resisting the unfamiliar feelings helps a lot. During Unraveling, it's good to respect that different interactions will cause unexpected feelings and responses. It's not a sign that we are unstable. I love C. S. Lewis's observation: "No one ever told me that grief felt so much like fear."[2]

Come to Terms with Negative Emotions

We don't have to justify our feelings to anyone, and we can let others have theirs as well. I mentioned earlier that it's important to let ourselves feel negative emotions instead of trying to explain them. When we try to make people see what we now see, we can get into trouble. Hopefully we have some people we can trust with these feelings, but we enter the danger zone when we try to explain ourselves to people who can't relate.

Jane is one of the wisest and most sincere Christ followers I have ever met. A dedicated wife and mother, she grew up in a home where negative emotions were quashed. She and her siblings were told to "play nice" and "don't come out of your room until you have a smile on your face." She then found a church system that replicated her past: it dictated that faithful followers should be happy and content at all times. Emotions weren't to be trusted, and the verse "The human heart is the most deceitful of all things, and desperately wicked" (Jeremiah 17:9) was embedded in her theology.

As Jane began Unraveling, anger welled up, but it's been hard for her to let it out freely without explanation or justification. Although she's learning to let herself feel and let her outside match her inside, it doesn't come easily—especially after being in a system where she says, "Robotic, spiritualized people were the ones admired."

Nathan is a quiet, steady advocate for the marginalized and poor in our neighborhood. When he unraveled, he described his feelings as "a deep, raw, bare-boned anger at being duped and used." Trying to make someone understand who has never been there is impossible, but he learned to own his feelings instead of push them down. When friends or family probed on specifics, he said, "I don't feel comfortable talking about that right now," "This isn't the time," or "I have other places that I am processing this and would like to keep it there." True, containing what feel like overwhelming emotions can be heavy lifting, but in the end it will protect our souls in a healthy way.

Consider the Possibility That Your Soul Is Not at Risk

Those of us from a more conservative background learned that unless we believed certain things, we were destined for hell. When we start Unraveling deeply held beliefs, the thought of going *too far, even for God to understand* is present. My friend and co-leader of our Walking Wounded online class, Phyllis Mathis, says all the time: "Remember, my friends, your souls are not in mortal danger."

I respect that this fear of eternal damnation doesn't just go away with these magic words, but if we can trust that God is big enough for this process, it will make all the difference. It's a stretch for some of us. You may be wondering, *Well, how do you know? How can you be so sure? What scriptures support that? What if you're wrong?*

I've asked all the same questions, and of course I can't give you a completely definitive answer. But I cling to this: if God is going to consign me to the pit of hell because I start asking some really important questions or let go of religiosity, then I'm not interested in that kind of God anyway. I still find great comfort in this passage:

> Can anything ever separate us from Christ's love? Does it
> mean he no longer loves us if we have trouble or calamity, or
> are persecuted, or hungry, or destitute, or in danger, or threat-
> ened with death?… I am convinced that nothing can ever
> separate us from God's love. Neither death nor life, neither
> angels nor demons, neither our fears for today nor our worries
> about tomorrow—not even the powers of hell can separate us
> from God's love. No power in the sky above or in the earth
> below—indeed, nothing in all creation will ever be able to
> separate us from the love of God that is revealed in Christ Jesus
> our Lord. (Romans 8:35, 38–39)

I do not believe our souls are in mortal danger, even if we walk away from everything we once knew. I believe God is big enough to handle it.

Accept That Some Relationships Will Fall Away

We are likely going to lose relationships with friends and family members over our Unraveling. The fundamental shift in how we view God, church, and the world can eliminate what we used to have in common.

Leslie, a curly haired, feisty twenty-something who exudes a vivid passion for justice and equality, was intimately involved in her church community, serving and giving her heart and time for many years. When she started to unravel, church members saw her as separated from them and told her they were praying for her to "come back soon." In other words, their relationship depended on her believing what they did. When Leslie could no longer ascribe to those things, not much was left. Often during Unraveling the divide becomes too wide.

I am a loyal friend, but learning to let go of certain friendships that couldn't hold my shifting faith has been a healthy practice. Sure, I am sad about some of the losses, but I am also trying to celebrate what we had and accept that sometimes friendships have a specific season. I may feel awkward when I see these people, but I no longer torture myself by thinking that I wasn't a good enough friend or I didn't try or pray hard enough to keep the relationship intact. Sometimes, we've just got to let them go in order to free ourselves.

Make Time for Safe, Life-Giving Friends

While some relationships won't survive our changing faith, hopefully we'll hold on to a few—or form new ones—that will help sustain us. Unraveling is too lonely without at least a few people to be free and honest with. You might be feeling abandoned right now, realizing that you don't have relationships in your life. The possibility of making new ones might also feel elusive. Safe relationships aren't easy to create, and sometimes we have to be really imaginative. Online communities and relationships can be surprisingly helpful and are fairly easy to form. It's also true that many of us just don't have the time. We are busy with real life and work, and taking time to hang out with friends and talk about faith stuff feels like a luxury. It's not. It's time well spent.

Treasure Laughter

Laughter really is the best medicine. Part of what got us into our faith mess in the first place was far too much seriousness. Having fun is so good for our souls. Go to funny movies, watch comedies on TV, hang out with silly friends. I have found so much healing in satire and humor. Laughing together about the ridiculousness of life lightens the load.

Practice Serenity

My mom went to Al-Anon when I was a kid, so we had plaques everywhere in our house with these important words: "God, grant me the serenity to accept the things I cannot change, courage to change the things I can, and wisdom to know the difference." When I started working the 12 Steps years ago to uproot my codependence and resolve the fallout of being an adult child of an alcoholic, it returned as a very comforting and powerful prayer to me. In the Unraveling process, it's important to get clear on what is beyond us: what we cannot change, or what we cannot expect from other people or our former faith systems. Words like those in the Serenity Prayer help us focus on what we can indeed change or work toward, what is within our control. We have a Wednesday evening group called House of Refuge that meets at our house. It is filled with a wonderful mix of faith shifters and men and women who understand the 12 Steps. As these worlds collide, the common ground is sharing our own story and respecting that we have the power to make choices that can lead us toward bitterness and anger—or freedom and hope.

Try Experiencing God in New Ways

One of the most distressing parts of this process was finding that all my old spiritual tricks (reading my Bible, journaling, doing a focused study, intentionally praying) stopped working. As I shifted and unraveled, I felt dead to things that once made me feel alive. When the place we used to go to for comfort is gone, we can feel lonely. Part of the journey has been learning to notice God's movement in my life and in the world through songs, people, experiences, movies, art, bizarre interactions, random scriptures, and other creative ways that I hadn't considered before. As I opened my heart, eyes, and ears to fresh ways of noticing God, and remained curious about all kinds of possibilities, my soul felt more tended to and less abandoned.

Trust the Process

When we are Unraveling, we can feel as though the darkness is endless. How long must we suffer? While some of what we hold dearly is indeed gone forever, over time we will find that what's left is enough and that we actually become more secure and stable than we might expect. We discover we don't have to go back to where we were to find strength again, regardless of how many people believe that Returning is our best hope. As we walk forward in the dark, light begins to creep in and then gets brighter over time, and our spiritual lives and practices take completely different forms.

Swear If It Helps!

You might cringe at this recommendation, and that's okay. You don't have to use this soul-care skill, but some need it, especially if they've tried to be holy for way too long. Honestly, one of the best things that ever happened to me was becoming free enough to let myself swear when I found the right word for the feelings. As a consummate Christian good girl, I held in so many emotions for so long that my soul was completely locked up. A significant part of my healing has come through becoming free, not just to use certain choice words, but to openly reveal what I'm actually thinking and feeling.

Be Selective in What You Read

It's important to choose wisely which blogs and books you read. During my Unraveling, I used to torture myself looking at certain websites, like my old church's blog. Every time I did, it would rip up my soul during a time when I needed more soothing and less angst. We may need to unfriend people on Facebook if seeing their religious and political posts are painful reminders. We might reconsider which posts to comment on because of the likelihood we will get sucked into a joy-robbing conversation instead of a life-giving one.

Be Selective About Which Events You Attend

This can be complicated when friends are still part of the systems we left, but it's a reality we have to live with. I have been invited to parties, weddings, and events where I knew I would be surrounded by too many unsafe people, so I made the difficult but healthy decision not to go. In certain groups we will get into conversations that will put us on the defensive. Of course, I have had to push through and attend a few events because they were special ones that I just couldn't miss, but I did put a strategy in place before I went (make sure Jose was with me, have a friend sit next to me, or have a reason to leave early). These small steps of taking good care of myself did not come naturally, but I keep discovering their value.

Resist the Temptation to Compare Yourself to Others

Comparing will harm us. We can look at people who are happy in the churches or faith systems we were part of and center our energies on what's wrong with us. We can look at others who are Unraveling too and think we're not doing it as smoothly or gracefully as they are. We can make up all kinds of expectations for ourselves during Unraveling that will do nothing but rob us of peace. We expect ourselves not to be mad anymore, not to get defensive when people bring up our shifts, or not to say anything negative about church in mixed company. When these things seep out, we feel shame for not being better yet. Letting go of comparisons is a lifelong process, but it's critically important during the tender process of deconstructing our faith.

Avoid Big Triggers If Possible

Sometimes this isn't possible, and we will wind up in a situation or conversation that trips all of our internal wires and makes us feel crazy. Still, we can find plenty of ways to make good choices and avoid places and people that will probably end up harming our souls. If trying to sit through a church service makes you nuts, don't go. If you have a partner who really wants you to attend with him or her, then consider ways to avoid the parts that are hardest. My friend Lynda would go to church with her family, but as soon as the music was over she would go sit in the lobby and drink coffee during the sermon because she just couldn't take it. She knew what things upset her and did what she could to avoid them.

Find what does bring life and practice it! Rumi, a Sufi mystic and poet, says, "When you do things from your soul, you feel a river moving in you, a joy."[3] Consider what is helpful to you, what you might add to the suggestions I've listed, what you keep learning along the way.

NURTURE LIFE-GIVING ACTS

Life in the spiritual desert of Unraveling requires water, rest, and food. As I let go of many old practices that stopped working, I intentionally worked at letting go of the guilt or "unspiritualness" I felt for not using them anymore. Then I began to experiment with things I do like to do. My criteria was asking myself, *Does this help me feel more peace, love, hope, joy, and/or rest?* Some of the practices I still try on this bumpy road include:

- lighting candles (lots of them)
- watching movies
- turning off the radio in my car and putting my cell phone in the back seat
- taking walks in the rain or sun or snow
- making time for friends who make me laugh
- reading only fiction
- reflecting on art or poetry
- writing
- water skiing
- hiking

I spent some time with a spiritual director too. Such people can be very helpful for people navigating a rocky faith shift. Spiritual directors usually have no vested interest in a particular congregation or denomination but are trained to be wise, compassionate, and challenging companions for people in their unique spiritual journeys. They are excellent guides to help shed baggage and discover ways to travel lighter in our relationship with God. You can find them in many Catholic or Episcopal churches or through local spiritual directors' networks (see the Resources section). They tend to be inclusive, gentle, wise, and patient, understanding the messiness and intricacies of an evolving faith.

Overall, I've tried to integrate the spiritual and the secular so they aren't so separate. It leaves room to experience God in the midst of the ordinary. Using my body more instead of only my head or heart has also been extremely transforming.

Other people I know decided to:

- take up dancing
- enroll in a nonreligious class
- begin painting again
- journal
- read a completely different translation of the Bible
- close their Bibles and read books that their former church told them were taboo
- enter therapy
- experiment with spiritual practices they had never considered before (meditation, centering prayer, Taizé)

What's life-giving for you? Part of our healing is to be brave enough to try things that feel foreign, scary, and even bizarre. Even if it takes awhile to find new habits and practices, each of us is filled up in unique and creative ways. Your challenge during Unraveling is to find practices that work for you. You will sometimes feel guilty, sacrilegious, and even stupid. Push through these blocks because the alternatives—shutting down your heart completely or going back to Egypt—are not viable options.

Remember, these are not just good things to do because someone else says they are. They are what will help sustain your soul during the arduous work of Unraveling. They are not selfish or ungodly. Often they are necessary for our souls' survival.

Questions for Personal or Group Reflection

1. At the beginning of this chapter, Kelly says, "I'm tired of talking, tired of processing, tired of feeling this way." When it comes to your Unraveling process, do you feel the same way? If not, what do you feel instead?

2. On a scale of 1 to 10 (1 being easy and 10 being hard), how difficult is it for you to take good care of your soul? Why?

3. This chapter includes a list of things that can help you make it through Unraveling. Which of these do you find most helpful? Why? Which is the hardest for you to apply?

4. Included in the list are several things to avoid during Unraveling. Which of these resonate with you the most? What else do you try to avoid?

5. What are some simple practices that bring you life? What are some of the obstacles to including them in your life? What can you do to make more time for them?

It's a Lot to Lose

*I lost a theology that once made sense. I lost hope
and trust in God and people. I lost a sense of
rightness to the universe. I lost direction and
purpose. And that's the short list.*

—Marshall

In our Walking Wounded online class, the level of honesty that emerges is astounding. Marissa, a participant from a small conservative church, found herself alone, single, and lost as her faith began to unravel. Once a faithful Bible study leader and Sunday school teacher, she describes Unraveling this way: "It's like a death or divorce, after which nothing will ever be the same. It's also a kind of grief that others don't understand because there's no memorial service, no divorce decree, no tangible moment to mourn. To me, it feels like I've lost everything, but others can't seem to figure out what all the fuss is all about."

During the class, we encourage people to allow themselves to feel their losses instead of minimizing their feelings or blaming others. Each person's experience is unique, and some aren't as drastic as Marissa's, but there's no way to get around painful emotions in Unraveling.

When it comes to issues of transformation, the principle of "Pay now or pay later—with interest" applies. If we push down our feelings and try to skim over them, eventually the feelings will ooze out, but with greater force that results in even more collateral damage, affecting our spouse, kids, and work as well as our physical health. Henri Nouwen says it beautifully: "Every time there are losses there are choices to make. You choose to live your losses as passages to anger, blame, hatred, depression, and resentment, or you choose to let these losses be passages to something new, something wider, something deeper."[1] Part of moving toward renewal and change is to acknowledge our losses. This is not so we can feel worse about our situation but so we can own it and find hope. We can eventually use these things as passages to something new, wider, and deeper.

Some of our losses are very specific and tangible: "I lost my church," "I lost my ministry position," or "I lost a specific relationship or my community of friends." Others are far more intangible, which make their impact even sneakier. Even though intangible losses might be a little harder to pin down, they often cause the greatest pain. To lose your sense of security, your passion for anything related to God, or your ability to respect people in authority or to trust your instincts —these aren't small things.

I can't say it enough: our spirituality and the ways we live it out are integral parts of our souls. When we lose them, it is like a death. People who haven't lost them can't understand, but those of us who have definitely know the feeling.

NAMING WHAT'S REALLY HAPPENING

Sue Monk Kidd shares some radical faith shifts in her book *The Dance of the Dissident Daughter*. As she began to recognize the disconnect between her conservative faith system and the feelings and questions in her heart, she began to speak up about it. Almost every time, she met with some form of resistance that caused her to doubt herself and minimize the struggle. She says, "Trivializing our experience is a very old and shrewd way of controlling ourselves. We do it by censoring our expressions of truth or viewing them as inconsequential. We learned the technique from a culture that has practiced it like an art form."[2] It makes sense. Most of us didn't come from faith systems that let us freely feel or say what we needed to. This is what makes faith shifts so uncomfortable.

Most of us tend to swing between two extremes with the pain of Unraveling. We either minimize the impact, or we end up deconstructing completely, which consumes every aspect of our lives. It's hard to live in the middle.

I am an expert at minimizing. I know how to gloss over pain and take the blame, to do almost anything not to feel hard feelings. My pull-myself-up-by-my-bootstraps skills usually come back to bite me. One of the hardest parts of my spiritual journey has been acknowledging how much I have truly lost over the years through this stripping process. It's easy to look at my life now and see how much I've gained. It's true, I am freer and healthier than I've ever been. But I still lost much of what held me together for so long. People, places, and beliefs that buoyed me are now completely gone.

Many of us are already in touch with our losses. They are on the tip of our tongues or we have been saying them out loud for a while. Others may have a tougher time acknowledging them and feel shame. Part of surviving Unraveling, as I've mentioned, is acknowledging losses in safe places —with trusted friends, therapists, spiritual directors, mentors, healing groups, or transformational communities—where grief is allowed. Naming losses, while difficult, validates something essential in our souls. It gives us the ability to say, "Oh yeah, that was really hard. I miss that. I miss them. I miss God. I'm so sad. It hurts."

DJ, Marshall, and Jane connected online through my blog and shared a common experience of deep loss during Unraveling. DJ describes the breadth of loss: "I lost almost everything. I lost my dreams and plans for the future. I lost my job, the ability to provide for my family, and I almost lost my marriage." Marshall lost direction and purpose and the ability to trust God and people. Jane lost her faith in leadership, longtime friends in community, and the perceived safety of a church family.

Some things I have lost over time related to faith and church:

- several extremely important friendships
- a well-paying ministry job
- my innocence
- my confidence
- my trust in almost any kind of leadership
- the ability to experience a spiritual high
- the freedom to sit in church and participate without critique and cringing
- core theological beliefs about God, Jesus, and the Bible
- desire and passion for the Bible

Consider for a moment what you may have lost. They probably fall into these three major categories—certainty and beliefs, relationships and structures, and identity and purpose.

Depending on your experience, you may lose more in one of these categories than others, but I think everyone loses some of all three. These losses are intertwined. As you identify and acknowledge what you've lost, understand that you are in good company.

WHAT USED TO SEEM CERTAIN

You may relate to what Rachel Held Evans, a popular faith blogger I mentioned earlier, says in her compelling memoir, *Evolving in Monkey Town*. She writes about Adele, who "describes fundamentalism as holding so tightly to your beliefs that your fingernails leave imprints on the palm of your hand." Do you know this feeling? Rachel says, "I was a fundamentalist not because of the beliefs I held but because of how I held them: with a death grip. It would take God himself to finally pry some of them out of my hands."[3] In Shifting, we might still have the energy or passion to try to hold on to our beliefs. In Unraveling, though, we actually watch what slips through our hands even when we try to grasp it again.

I recently asked thirty men and women to share beliefs they've lost as they've shifted and unraveled. Here's a sample:

- certainty about what is actually "God's truth"
- what it means to be "saved"
- perspectives on hell
- the need for substitutionary atonement
- the sovereignty of God
- "Christian" worldviews
- the ability to feel connected to God through the Scriptures
- a clarity on who God is
- belief in the inerrancy of the Bible
- Christianity as "the only way"
- specific roles for men and women
- what is sin
- God's maleness
- the Creation story as we were taught it
- the black-and-whiteness of God's Word

- the divinity of Jesus
- Jesus as the only way to God
- God's "political beliefs"
- the hierarchical structures of church
- the value or purpose of church

These are scary things to lose, especially when people around us are still holding tightly to them. Let's look at a few of these more closely.

"I'm Not Sure How to Read the Bible Anymore"

The issue of the inerrancy of the Bible is significant. The Bible has been called the "Word of God." Losing certainty in it can feel extra confusing to many people who were part of fundamentalist churches because everything they learned was based on it. They've never allowed the possibility that the Word of God might be something larger than the words of God. As they take their belief about the Bible out of the Jenga game, it can feel like the missing piece that will make the entire tower topple. If the Bible isn't the highest form of authority, what is?

Phyllis Tickle, author of *The Great Emergence,* has written extensively about the significant shift in Christianity and her belief that we are in the midst of another Reformation.[4] We are shifting from the Bible as our ultimate authority to the Holy Spirit as primary authority. These aren't clean, simple shifts. Generations of people have been taught the absolute authority of the Scriptures. Calling them into question has caused more than a few small rifts between denominations—it's started a Christian culture war. It's being fought on Facebook, in blogs, and elsewhere on the Internet. Many unravelers feel fine sharing publicly about changing views about the Bible, but many more people don't want to for fear of backlash. It's why so many of us go underground during faith shifts.

Recently I participated in some extremely difficult and intense conversations about homosexuality. The fascinating part of the conversation was how passionate people are about "But the Bible says…" I kept saying, "Yes, I know you are sure that is what those words mean, but others of us see the same words and draw a different conclusion."

As I wrestled in these conversations, I felt, at a new and profound level, how vulnerable we feel when we lose our certainty about the Scriptures. I was uncomfortably reminded that in certain circles I am viewed as someone who doesn't highly value the Bible. If you have a conservative faith background, you probably have a similar painful story related to the fallout of losing your "biblical truth."

"I Feel Increasingly Unorthodox About Orthodoxy"

I met Missy after she heard about the Refuge and wondered if it might be a place of healing for her after an unexpected divorce. As we shared stories at a local coffee shop, quiet strength and deep wisdom oozed out through her tears. For Missy, Unraveling occurred when her marriage imploded. After years of faithful service, she was alone with nowhere to go. She had a much longer list of what she didn't believe than what she did. The losses felt overwhelming and she was looking for something constant in a sea of unknowns. Missy says,

> The loss of certainty brought anxiety, grief, and a desperate
> feeling to try to find something, anything, that was certain.
> I would take walks and note all of the things that would
> certainly be the same—the sun would always come up, the
> leaves would always turn beautiful colors, my mother and
> father would always love me, babies would always be born,
> and on and on. It brought some comfort.

When so much is stripped away, we need to somehow find a sense of mooring.

On one Easter Sunday I wrote a post for my blog called "When Easter Is Hard." I realized that though I had carved out a place to safely celebrate Easter at the Refuge, many friends were sad, lonely, and feeling weird that day. I wanted to acknowledge their pain. Whether we are Protestant, Catholic, charismatic, conservative, or liberal, Easter is embedded in our culture. For many of us, it used to be our favorite holiday, our church's big hurrah, but after a faith shift it's become a disorienting day where the reality of everything we've lost becomes most evident. So while Facebook, Twitter, and every Christian church on the planet is abuzz with "He is risen!" and "Hallelujah!" we're not sure what to make of the resurrection anymore, what *the blood of Jesus* actually means, and why God's story—which used to feel so simple and clear—now feels bizarre, inconsistent, and confusing.

"My Feelings Are a Mess"

While some people miss their crumbled beliefs, others get really angry. When he began Unraveling from core beliefs, Miguel wasn't just mad at Christianity, the system he had served for most of his adult life. He found he was actually "pissed at a God that I no longer believed in." That alone is confusing. How do we yell and scream at someone or something we aren't even sure exists?

That reveals another belief many of us lose in the process of Unraveling: that there's a God who actually listens to and hears us. We may have spent years hearing how God knows our thoughts before we think them and that we should "pour our hearts out to Jesus," but during Unraveling we often lose confidence about who or what is on the other end of our cries, our prayers, our heart laments.

Our lists of lost certainty and beliefs may look different, but once these tightly held doctrinal beliefs and core values begin to dissolve, the next things we lose are friends, jobs, and the churches or groups we belonged to.

AND THEN THERE'S CHURCH...

Because our church structures are built so fervently on right belief, our church friends frequently can't handle our changes. Relationships we felt were based on intimate connection and deep love for each other actually were built upon function, conformity, and the comforts of shared belief. When we stop playing by the same rules, we end up not just on the sidelines but out of the game completely.

For her entire life, Elisa, a fiercely loyal mother of three, had been a key player in every church she attended. Because she was always serving and in leadership, it was hard to distinguish where the church ended and she started. They had been intimately entwined for as long as she could remember. Elisa knew that some of her questions and doubts might mean she couldn't lead certain groups any longer, but she wasn't prepared for rejection. "My understanding of church being a safe place for close, loving, healing, intimate relationships shattered. I felt like I'd been sold a lie. Church was not safe, and when I lost that, I lost all of it. That loss completely broke my heart."

Lauren's background was completely different, but she and Elisa could be soul sisters. Now an outspoken advocate for the LGBT community, Lauren was raised in a Catholic family but as an adult she was a faithful, consistent member of a nondenominational church. As she started to shift, she began to feel on the outs of many conversations. She'd show up at parties or events and realize that the things her friends and acquaintances were talking about didn't interest her anymore. Her desire to talk about religious or political issues in the same way had radically changed. Without those common beliefs to bind them together, she found nothing left to talk about.

Marco's passion for Jesus is tangible, and you can't help but feel the warmth of his bright eyes and wide smile. Shifting views were hard enough for the conservative church he was part of, but he did think that because he had been involved there for so long that he could hold on to his relationships. But when he ran into trouble with the law, those friends disappeared and he lost the community he had served and loved for many years. His pastor told him, "God forgives your sins, but he will never be able to use you again." The confidence Marco once had to lead crumbled.

When June, an avid gardener, advocate for the poor, and mother of three young sons, started Shifting, she and her husband took a break from serving in the church. For several years, they had led and organized all kinds of ministry teams. Now they began to feel a slow drift from friends. When they decided to take a more formal break from church, they realized that none of those relationships existed outside of their active involvement. June and her husband hadn't been people who just showed up on Sundays: they had offered countless hours over the years. Yet no one pursued them when they were gone. "It felt like finding out we were just being used for what we could do for the church instead of loved for being the church," June said.

I know this feeling well. When I exited the church that I had loved and served with all my heart, soul, and strength, not one person in leadership contacted me and asked how I was. People I had led with through some pretty intense times never even acknowledged I was gone. I kept wondering if they'd call, but they didn't.

When Kristin converted to Mormonism in high school, she went all in. Later, as a stay-at-home mom, she looked as if she had the perfect life: two beautiful kids and a charismatic, successful husband. In reality, though, she experienced incredible verbal and physical abuse. After a defining incident, Kristin ended up divorcing. It catalyzed a catastrophic unravel because she didn't lose just her marriage, she also lost her church. She became an outsider, not only with her church friends but with her grown children too, who were firmly entrenched in the Mormon church. Her questioning of the church's response to her abuse was too much for them, and they abandoned relationship with her. Kristin lost every single significant relationship and a sense of belonging that had sustained her for decades. She's still reeling.

Religious systems are strong. When people inside the systems don't play by the same rules, everything changes, and not in a good way. The relationships we once treasured slip away. Our ability to freely participate as a member in the groups, churches, and ministries either slowly or quickly evaporates. When our beliefs and then our relationships are gone, it's only natural that the next place we'd take a hit is in the core part of our souls—our identity and purpose.

WHO ARE WE NOW...REALLY?

When I first landed on the outside of church, I started an informal group called the Ex-Good-Christian Women's Breakfast Club. It was a way to bring some brave female friends together on a regular basis to share encouragement and support. Through the years, that group has been crucial to my healing because I can openly share what it feels like to lose the identity I had clung to for many years. Most of my former life was built upon people pleasing and performance. I was loved and accepted when I was doing, saying, and believing the right things. And because one of my biggest fears in this world was abandonment and rejection, I had an almost toxic addiction to keeping everyone around me happy.

After my faith free fall, the biggest loss was people's approval. When I started ranting about dysfunctional church systems and my evolving liberal theological perspectives, it wasn't some twisted experiment in being brave. It was part of shedding my identity and living with the painful consequences of that loss.

The cultures we come from are laden with powerful stereotypes about what is acceptable for both men and women. These expectations are crippling. Colleen, a middle-school teacher with a calm, peaceful spirit, sums it up well: "If I am not this good Christian woman, then who am I?" Many men are asking the same question about being a "good Christian man."

These are some identity questions people ask during Unraveling: Who are we when…

- we no longer believe the same things or remain part of a church?
- we don't lead or serve?
- people disapprove of us?
- family members are hurt, angry, or concerned that we no longer want to play church with them?
- we are no longer directly affiliated with a church or group?
- we stay home on Sundays, as most people do?
- we don't call ourselves Christians?
- our children aren't learning about God in church?

Really, all roads lead to *Who are we now that we've changed?*

Sophia was a professional counselor, teacher, elder, interim pastor, and church leader for most of her adult life. She always had a strong sense of calling to the church. The loss of her beliefs and structures led to a paralyzing identity crisis:

> When I no longer believed in preaching, I wondered what I was supposed to do with my desire to teach. When I lost my beliefs, I wondered what I would teach about. My life purpose came to a bewildering halt. I was burned out at work, done with church, and finished with Christianity. My sense of identity and purpose was completely gone.

Realizing she had invested decades of heart and soul in a system focused on looking and being good also completely deflated my friend Avery's identity. When her eyes opened to the hypocrisy and fakeness of many Christian churches, she had no place to feel secure anymore. She felt panicky and desperate to feel good about something. To fill the loss, she began immersing herself in her budding career. Avery is still navigating deep waters to discover her purpose in this world apart from her husband's pastoral position or her family of origin's rigid faith.

When I was on a big church staff, my marriage, children, and health directly suffered. The call felt so urgent and consuming, however, that I didn't even realize the damage until much later. God had felt incredibly alive and real to me during that season. But when I look back from a saner perspective, I feel conflicted about whether it was really God or my crazy desire to be part of a movement that aligned with my passions. My identity was being part of something special (the core message in the culture I was in) so when it was gone, I didn't only feel as though I wasn't special. I felt as though I was nothing—and maybe I had been living a big, fat, ugly lie.

I am glad I'm not the only one who has felt the sting of identity loss. June, a church-burnout with stunning green eyes and a mischievous spirit, says, "I used to have a really strong sense of calling to be involved in missions. Now I have a hard time knowing what to do with that calling." For many of us, the feelings aren't completely gone, but our ability to trust them after Unraveling becomes shaky.

Loss of identity is just as difficult for men as it is for women. Miguel, a gruff but tender firefighter, "mourned the loss of the person I had worked my whole adult life to become." Duncan, a military retiree and ordained minister transitioning to an entirely new career, describes his evolution of identity this way: "I went from enthusiastic follower, to church reformer, to broken pastor, to finally-at-peace nonbeliever."

IN MOTION TOWARD SOMETHING NEW

As we unravel we can notice our shifting identities over time. We have been the "lost sinner who becomes found" for a while, then transitioned into the "zealous new believer who is on fire for Jesus" until we became a "mature, Bible-believing Christian actively involved in church." We might now be "the misfit, the rabble-rouser, the project, or the disobedient one." Some women look back and see how much of their identity was tied up in being a "faithful wife" or "humble servant" or "loving Christian mother." Often our identities were tied up in predetermined roles that came with the culture. During Unraveling we can feel liberated because we know these roles need to go, but it's also unsettling to not have a clearly defined person to be afterward.

Where does the season of Unraveling eventually take us? I wish I could say that once we check off the list of what we lost and process it properly, we emerge right away on the other side of a faith shift, new and shiny, completely free of the trappings of the past. Unfortunately, Unraveling seems to be an ongoing and unpredictable part of faith shifting that doesn't always have a clear beginning or end. And while sometimes we can unravel all the way and still maintain some kind of connection with God and church, others of us end up losing our faith altogether.

That's why I call this next season Severing. It's a drastic word for a reason, but sometimes it's where a particular Unraveling leads. Not everyone experiences Severing. Some can begin to rekindle and rebuild faith directly after Unraveling (that's my experience, and the last section of this book is focused solely on Rebuilding), while others sever for different periods of time or possibly forever. Regardless, it's critical that we walk through the tender stage of Severing together because it's very real for many.

Questions for Personal or Group Reflection

1. What specific beliefs have you lost? A good way to start this list is with "I no longer believe…" or "I used to believe…" When you are done, take a little break and reflect on what it feels like to see these in black and white. I'd encourage you to share them out loud with someone you trust. It can be extremely helpful to acknowledge what's changed.

2. What relationships (individuals or groups) or structures (churches, groups, or ministries) have you lost during Unraveling? What are some of your feelings about these particular losses?

3. How have you lost some of your identity, passion, or purpose during Unraveling? What are some of your own "Who am I without..." questions? Describe what this loss of identity has been like for you.

4. Do you have a safe space to express these losses? If not, can you think of some possible options that might be a place to start?

Cutting Ties

The Stage of Severing

I didn't walk away from my spirituality. That would mean there was something to walk away from. Looking back, it's almost as if Jesus died or God moved away. Most of me didn't care if I ever heard from them again.

—MIGUEL

One morning Fiona, a former pastor's wife and respected Bible study leader, awoke with a disturbingly clear feeling that she had become an atheist. She had been in the midst of a massive faith shift for over a year and was exiting an extremely legalistic and rigid background. Her sister's homosexuality had rocked her faith and was a powerful catalyst for her Unraveling. As Fiona began to wrestle with God and the Scriptures, she came to believe that homosexuality wasn't a sin and ended up outside of the church for the first time in her life.

Since then Fiona has been considering whether or not God exists at all. And if he does, she's convinced he's not like the one she had learned about. She wants nothing to do with anything that smells of religiosity or bondage. Some days Fiona feels as though she's maybe more of an agnostic (someone who believes there is a God but without specific definitions or dogma), while other days she'd call herself a Christian agnostic, which to her means a belief in Jesus without any baggage of Christianity. Regardless of which label she wears on a particular day, the crucial truth she has needed to embrace for her healing is that she really is okay. No matter what she believes, she is going to be all right.

In the stage I call *Severing*, many cut ties with anything religious or church related. Again, not everyone severs. In fact, many people skip this stage altogether and move directly from Shifting to Unraveling to Rebuilding without such a harsh break. This Severing season may include embracing atheism and denouncing God altogether, or it may mean completely leaving Christianity and all of its trappings, at least temporarily. I love Anne Lamott's wise words in her book *Help, Thanks, Wow: The Three Essential Prayers,* "We learn through pain that some of the things we thought were castles turn out to be prisons, and we desperately want out, but even though we built them, we can't find the door."[1]

That's how Severing can feel. But we can rest in the waiting, in the unknowing, and live without God or spirituality for a while. In time, we may find that it's not the end of the world. For some, it's hard and painful, filled with angst and loneliness. For others, it can feel freeing, a place where they finally feel unhindered by the many chains that used to bind them. Some may stay severed forever, but far more men and women I know end up stopping there temporarily on their journey to a new place in their faith.

Here's where I'd put Severing on our faith evolution illustration:

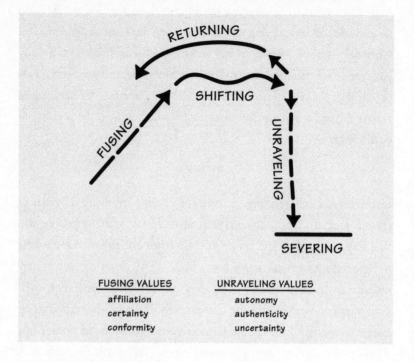

A fascinating thing that emerged from my interviews for this book was that most people said they never completely severed from God during their radical faith shifts. Yes, they cut ties to much of their past, but somehow a thread of belief in God remained. But that's not the case for everyone.

IT'S NOT GOOD OR BAD—IT'S JUST REAL

If you have been through this stage or find yourself there now, you've no doubt heard people label those who break relationship with God as *weak, self-centered, rebellious, dangerous,* or *prideful.* My advice: don't listen to them. These convenient judgments strike me as attempts to exert control and judgment over others. I think of Jesus's words in the Sermon on the Mount, reminding us to worry about the log in our own eye instead of focusing on the speck in our brother's. Honestly, I wonder how much of people's need to warn and admonish Severers is just a way to hide their own anxieties and fears beneath the guise of love.

I respect that the idea of Severing can make people feel extra anxious, but let me be clear: I am not promoting walking away from God. I'm not saying it's a good or bad thing; I'm saying it's a real thing. It's part of many people's faith evolution. If that's where we are, we need to let ourselves walk through this experience.

This is a time when we need to take care of our tender hearts. Severing can be like a spiritual cleanse, a chance to empty out all of the toxins that have built up over the years. When we've been through a war, our souls can be beat up and broken. Many have experienced spiritually abusive systems and been crushed under oppression, legalism, and religious control. Recovering from spiritual abuse is possible, but we may need a specific period where we disengage completely in order to heal. In other words, Severing can be a healthy protection mechanism that isn't about bitterness or anger, but actually about mending our souls. God is big enough for all the ways that we sever. And instead of fearing the process, we can respect that sometimes it's our best hope.

You may be finished believing there is a God. Or you may still believe God exists, even though you might cut off relationship for a while or even forever. Wherever you are, I respect your position. I have plenty of room in my heart, theology, and experience for atheism, even though that hasn't been my story. Many call themselves *agnostic, ex-Christians, spiritual but not religious, followers of Jesus, still Christians,* and a whole host of other identifiers. What we have in common is a deep desire to eventually move forward after the gut-wrenching seasons of Shifting and Unraveling.

CONCLUSIONS WE MIGHT COME TO

In many ways, Severing is about coming to specific conclusions after Unraveling, even if they are temporary, so we can find some peace. Although Severing looks different for each person, we can identify some core elements. See if any of these resonate for you:

"Maybe There Is No God"

When I was training to be a spiritual director at Denver Seminary, I loved studying the desert mothers and fathers of our faith. I always appreciated St. John of the Cross, a Spanish mystic, priest, and church reformer in the Carmelite order in the 1500s. Because of his public statements related to church reform, he was imprisoned, tortured, and placed in extreme isolation, and he almost died. He is most famous for writing a piece titled "The Dark Night of the Soul," in which he describes a real and pervasive absence of God for a period of time. In St. John's theology, God's absence was intentional to teach him something important and to purify his soul.

For some, Severing can look and feel like a dark night of the soul, where after shedding all of our formerly held beliefs, we are quite certain that we've either been completely abandoned by God or that maybe there is no God at all. Chloe, an energetic and thoughtful children's therapist, describes her Severing as a time of "spiritual anorexia." After becoming a born-again Christian, she gorged on any "spiritual food" she could get her hands on. Over time, though, and after a disorienting season of Unraveling, Chloe became spiritually emaciated but has no desire to eat anything. The thought of any kind of spiritual nourishment is repellent. She's honest, though, and says that even though she doesn't want to eat, she is indeed hungry for something. In some ways, hunger can make Severing even worse for those who long for connection and renewal but have no ability or will to receive it.

Even though Miguel says emphatically he is done with God, he's honest about how painful it was to come to that conclusion. A strong, confident man, he admits he cried many times as he watched his faith slip away. The word *severing* can make us think of losing a leg or an arm, but Miguel felt it was even far more drastic than that—everything and anything related to faith was completely gone. He didn't lose just Christianity, he also lost a sense that there was really a God, although he hasn't ruled out that there's something spiritual about the universe he can't explain.

When I first met Andrew, a young, talented artist, he was making videos for Christian organizations. Even though he had exited traditional church, he still was on the fringes of several alternative-faith communities. Now he's decided to leave altogether. Andrew's Severing was far more gradual than Miguel's, and he didn't even notice it until it had already happened. One day he realized, *I don't believe in Jesus. I'm not sure there is a God.* Today he says he is "agnostic with atheistic tendencies." After being part of Christian ministry for many years, he is sometimes confused about whether or not he should share his revelation. He's chosen to share selectively, depending on how it comes up, but what has been most freeing for him is that he is not angry or bitter anymore. Andrew's Severing did not feel messy or violent. He slowly and methodically left Christian spirituality, and when he finally accepted where he had ended up, it felt natural and brought him deep peace.

Scarlett was always an individualist who struggled to fit into Christianity for most of her adult life. A scientist with an innate psychological and spiritual bent, she did sincerely believe but a part of her always held back from God. After a long Unraveling, she ended up with clarity that she was indeed completely severed: "I don't try to rationalize it to anyone or figure it out for myself. I just woke up in the morning and knew that it looked exactly as it did the mornings that I woke up believing in God."

Many people experiment with atheism as a portion of their faith shifting. Some embrace it forever. I know the words *agnostic* or *atheist* can be associated with mortal sins. What's most important is to respect that sometimes, at the end of Unraveling, we may end up losing all belief in God. It doesn't mean you'll stay there for the rest of your life. New fires can light inside of your soul. If not, that's fine too.

"I Think Some Kind of God Exists, but..."

After Unraveling, many people become agnostics or spiritual but not religious (SBNR). SBNRs still hold a core belief in the existence of God but are unable to articulate a clear theological framework in which to place God. They believe in a "higher power," as Alcoholics Anonymous teaches, or a "God of the universe" or a "creator," but they have no language to define exactly what that God is like.

In her book *Christianity After Religion,* Diana Butler Bass writes about people's responses to the words *spirituality* and *religion.* People associated spirituality with "experience, connection, transcendence, searching, intuition, prayer, meditation, open, wisdom, 12-steps, inclusive, doubt." Religion brought words such as "institution, organization, rules, order, dogma, authority, beliefs, buildings, structure, hierarchy, orthodoxy, boundaries, certainty."[2] Many people who sever are finished with the words on the religion list, but their hearts are still stirred by the words on the spirituality side. They want God but not religion.

My two oldest children, now young adults, fall into this category. Their conservative Christian school experience and the rigid obedience of our early years really did a number on their faith. That is one of my deepest regrets. We fully bought into the conservative evangelical system during their crucial formative years, and they paid the price. Today they wouldn't say, "I am severed," but while they have no interest in anything religious, they do believe in some kind of God. Just about everything they once believed unraveled.

As a parent, I feel responsible for some of the damage done, but I also feel a great peace that I don't have to manage or navigate their journeys. I can trust them and God. I respect their decisions. Beating myself up about it won't help anything. My sense is that someday, when they are ready, they will decide not to remain ambivalent and engage with some of their feelings about God at an even deeper level.

"I'm Done with Christianity, not God"

While some people walk away from faith completely, many more don't sever from God but rather from the conception of God expressed in their former faith systems. They have a strong desire to shed connection with the churches of their youth and cut ties to the baggage associated with Christianity as organized religion. Really, it's a rejection of the God they've always known.

Because Lissa, a local potter and doting grandmother, was a dedicated Christian for many years, her former colleagues in faith keep trying to woo her back. They sent a sometimes subtle, often direct, message that who she was wasn't okay. But the truth is that she's been happier in the past few years since she severed her ties with Christianity than she's ever been in her life. Shame has lost much of its grip, she is creating deeply healing art, and she goes to the movies every Sunday morning with a few friends who call it the best form of church they've ever experienced. Counter to everything she was taught, Lissa needed to reject her old concept of God in order to get to a new place. Her head was tired of overthinking, and her heart was worn out from feeling broken. Lissa says the greatest transformation has come through letting go:

> I just don't know what a faith expression looks like for me anymore. I've taken a hiatus from trying to decide what I believe, because so much of what I considered faith was just a collection of theories about God. Real faith is something else entirely, and I'd like to find ways to experience the essence of faith in new ways. For a while I seriously wondered if there is a God. I tried hard not to believe in God at all, but I just couldn't pull it off. I couldn't tell you who God is, or how God really operates in the universe anymore, but I can't shake the belief that there is one.

Wrestling with these issues related to God is not heresy—rather, it can be a spiritual act. Lissa was a Christian for more than thirty years, but after Unraveling, she completely severed from the brand of Christianity she had lived. Author Peter Rollins writes,

> [Paul] Tillich argued that a serious rejection of God (rather than a mere lack of interest in the subject) is a deeply sacred act. For when someone rejects the notion of God because of the wars that have been fought over that name, as well as the abuse, the fundamentalism and the ecological destruction that is bound to so much religion, they are demonstrating a profound concern for both people and the planet…. The stronger their attack [against God] the more care and concern

they are showing. In this very assault they are thus asserting, in a direct and visceral way, a commitment to the protection and promotion of life. The result is a proclamation of the sacred that is birthed from the same mother as the message found on the lips of the various poets and prophets in the Biblical text.[3]

Nathan, deeply immersed in ministry for most of his adult life, says, "I want nothing to do with the God represented by my former perspective. That has felt liberating, but it's also disorienting." We often can't cultivate a new image of God when we're still holding on to the old one. Part of Severing can be choosing intentionally to cut off relationship with the old God while hoping a new one might eventually emerge.

My friend Jane uses trapeze imagery to illustrate faith shifting, and it works for Severing too. As we let go of our past conceptions and experiences with God, we have to live in the scary in-between where we are hanging in limbo, wondering if a new bar will swing for us to grab onto. Until then, we live separated from our old images of God and in the empty space that has replaced them.

For others, Severing might not look as drastic or risky. Darrell, a therapist and former worship leader, says that his Severing was "gradually coming to believe in an entirely different God than I used to. Now I feel I know very little about what there is to know about the true God, and I'm learning to accept that reality. I no longer believe there are simple answers to complex questions, but I'm still sure that God is somehow good."

Meg, once a full-time youth minister with a popular worldwide organization, can't call herself a Christian anymore, but she can't completely shake a belief in God. She likes Jesus's ways but isn't sure whether the resurrection occurred. She has distanced herself from organized religion and Christianity, but she can't go as far as to doubt God's existence entirely.

Meg's Severing was a relief, but it has created a deep loneliness too. Some of her friends started to shift with her but returned to their churches or have held on to far more beliefs than she did. Meg finds that she is on the fringes of even the most edgy conversations about faith. While she doesn't know what the future related to her faith will bring, she does know she is completely done with the limiting ties of her past.

I once argued with a friend who said he was no longer a Christian. I said it was just semantics, that he was leaving Christianity as an organized religion but not leaving Jesus altogether. I was wrong. I needed to listen to him and honor his words instead of imposing mine on him. He said emphatically, "Kathy, I'm done. I'm not a Christian anymore." I learned something important: some people cut themselves off from Christianity and Jesus altogether, while others sever from Christianity and still hold on to Jesus. At least for now, my friend is finished with Jesus too.

Living in that crazy space where we let ourselves find our own way in Severing is not easy. My friend Evan hangs out with homeless people in Southern California and hasn't set foot in a church in years, but he has found life and purpose being the hands and feet of Jesus in a completely different context. He severed from the institution but hasn't severed from Jesus. Again, there is no template on how exactly to sever.

"To Save My Soul, I Need to Let Go of My Faith"

Spiritual abuse is rampant, and the stories I hear about emotional manipulation and distortions of God make me want to scream. My heart hurts at the magnitude of damage done in Jesus's name. One of the hardest things for most spiritual abuse survivors to do is to let go completely of faith for a while. Usually people who have endured spiritual abuse were part of systems that required an "all-in" kind of commitment, so survivors are often some of the most sincere Christians I have ever met. Their heads and hearts are so traumatized by their experience that they can't do what some shifters do and transition from Unraveling into Rebuilding with very little effort. They have too much pain to navigate, and often their best hope is to take a break from God for a while.

This is a lot to ask of people who were so deeply dedicated to their faith. I am not saying it's for everyone, but if you are a spiritual-abuse survivor, sometimes it's the best hope for healing. Trying to build a bridge to something new is too anguishing. A better alternative is to bomb the bridge completely and trust that eventually you'll either learn to swim or find the materials and tools you need to build something new. Severing for a while will open a space to learn how to be human apart from toxic religious systems. You may need time to focus internally and to feel things that were prohibited before. I've had many friends who have severed temporarily to heal from abuse.

Alexa, a single mom with grown children, lived in an abusive church system for many years. A once-faithful follower of Jesus, she now is spending loads of money on therapy and trying to figure out how to move forward. She put her toe in the water at the Refuge a few times, but it was too traumatic to try to reengage with God or people yet. Alexa needs a long sabbatical where all things related to God, Jesus, and the Holy Spirit are completely off the table. She loosely hangs on to relationships with a few of us at the Refuge, and we may be a conduit of hope in the future. But for now, she needs to stay in a neutral space and gain the healing she needs.

TOWARD SOMETHING LASTING

There are other distinct examples of ways people sever after Unraveling. You may be in the midst of yours right now or remember when you were there. Again, not all of us sever, and many are able to unravel and move toward Rebuilding something new without going through this season. If you've recognized yourself in this chapter, my hope is that over time you can find the good in this process and the relief, clarity, and freedom that bring deep and lasting healing.

Questions for Personal or Group Reflection

1. How would you draw or describe Severing?

2. How do you relate to this particular stage of Severing? Do you recognize any of the symptoms of Severing in your experience?

3. When you consider the broad categories of Severing—*atheism, agnosticism, spiritual but not religious, done with Christianity but still a follower of Jesus, or taking an extended break from God*—what sounds closest to where you are today? (It doesn't have to be any of these particular categories.)

4. On a scale of 1 to 10 (1 being easy and 10 being hard), how difficult is this season of Severing? Using the same scale, how easy or hard do you think it is for the people around you to see you severed?

5. How have people around you reacted to your decisions related to your faith choices? How has that affected you? What do you wish they would try to understand?

Against All Odds, New Life Springs Up

The Stage of Rebuilding

I am left with fewer truths, but they are clearly deeper.

—June

Katherine, a blogger and compassionate friend to men and women recovering from spiritual abuse, exited not only an abusive church, but her emotionally abusive family as well. Her journey has been traumatic, but she is slowly healing. She shed many beliefs and lost significant relationships during a difficult Unraveling yet retained a deep sense of God's love for her. She feels stuck between two worlds, out of one but not yet in another. She left church but longs for a community to belong to again. Her fragile hope keeps beckoning her forward: "I do know that through tears and confusion, fears and anger, I just need to not give up. I need to keep moving, even when I'm not sure what that even means or looks like."

Katherine is someone with an unraveled faith who is ready to rebuild. When we first fused, we had a sense of wonder and innocence that we can never fully recapture. But now, after our beliefs have come undone, it's as if we wear different glasses that color our views on issues of faith and church. Deciding whether to risk our hearts with God again makes us feel vulnerable. Actively pursuing justice, mercy, and creativity feels extremely brave. The idea of trying church community again requires even more courage.

Several years ago when I wrote a blog series called "Rebuilding After Deconstructing," some common themes emerged. People who responded to the series expressed a range of reactions:

- feeling uncertain about where to find help or gather hope to revive their faith
- a deep desire not to leave faith altogether but to discover possibilities of connecting with God in new ways
- a desire for *freedom, mystery,* and *diversity*—instead of *certainty, conformity,* or *affiliation*—to be guiding values
- a longing to hope, dream, and serve again
- a craving for some form of community or church experience that is safe, healing, and challenging

Hope still exists when all appears lost. A shifter's overarching desire here is not to leave faith altogether but to rebuild something. This time, we can reengage with greater wisdom, maturity, and authenticity. We can color outside the lines and create something more fluid, creative, and artful. We can rediscover old spiritual practices and bravely develop new ones. We can begin to rebuild an active, passionate, simpler faith with fewer pieces but more depth.

Countless memoirs, blogs, and online forums center on deconstructing our faith, but few tangible tools exist for building something new. Because people land in divergent places after exiting the familiar, it's difficult to know who's ready for Rebuilding and who isn't...who isn't sure where they are and who's ready to reengage after a long season of disconnection…who's finished with church completely and who wants to try again…who's done with being angry and who still needs to be. We're all in such tender places during faith shifting.

We need tools, ideas, and practices that can help us navigate the uncharted territory of Rebuilding our fractured faith. We need comrades for the journey who relate to the feelings of being mocked for going to church again or understand what it's like to discover renewed life and purpose outside of organized religion. We need inspiration and hope even though we might not know where we are going. There is indeed a path to loosely follow that might help fan some of our desires into flame. There is life on the other side of a faith shift. It's much harder to define, describe, and live out than anything we've previously experienced—but it's possible.

In fact, our desire for freedom, diversity, and mystery in our relationship with God and the world will guide us into uncharted territories. We will try things we've never tried before. We will engage with people we've never engaged with before. We will notice God in places we never saw him before. We will love in ways we never did before. We will become freer.

This is the last addition to our faith evolution diagram. See the following page for how I picture Rebuilding.

The line representing Rebuilding is squiggly for a reason. Gone are the straight ascending lines of Fusing, the wobbly ups and downs of Shifting, the clear, direct path back to Returning, the crazy downward drop of Unraveling, or the harsh disconnection of Severing. Rebuilding means we won't be the same, and it probably looks different from many other lives around us. It won't fit into a simple formula or follow a specific pattern. Instead, it will be a revived, imaginative way of living that will emerge and change over time.

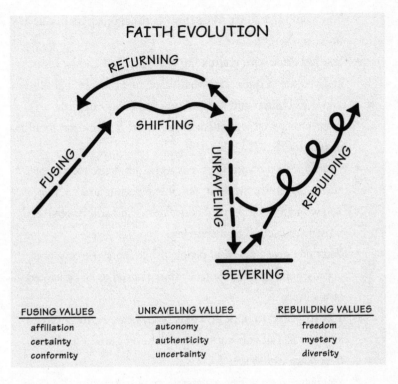

FAITH EVOLUTION

RETURNING

FUSING

SHIFTING

UNRAVELING

REBUILDING

SEVERING

FUSING VALUES	UNRAVELING VALUES	REBUILDING VALUES
affiliation	autonomy	freedom
certainty	authenticity	mystery
conformity	uncertainty	diversity

SIGNS OF LIFE

There are no hard and fast rules for knowing you are ready for Rebuilding your faith after Unraveling. Still, reflecting on my own journey and the many conversations I've had with other faith shifters, here are some ideas you might have in common with other Rebuilders:

- You are tired of being angry at the church.
- You miss God and long for ways to engage spiritually again.
- Your loneliness is too exhausting, and you need to find new friends with whom to share real life.
- You're through grieving your past and want to look toward the future.

- You would like to try some fresh spiritual practices but have no idea where to start.
- You feel done with church but not with God and/or Jesus, and you aren't quite sure what shape that takes in real life.
- You miss church and want to find some form of faith community that will quench your thirst for connection and inspiration.
- You want to use your gifts, passions, and desire for justice and mercy in the world in tangible ways but aren't sure how.
- You wonder what parts of your faith might still be alive and if they are enough to sustain you.
- You don't give a rip what people think about you anymore because your spiritual journey doesn't need to be explained or justified.
- You are afraid to hope and open your heart again to God and others, but you know you will never get to a healthier, freer place unless you do.
- You want to grow in a new way, not only for yourself but so you can pass on something of substance to your children too.

Do any of these sound like your experience? What would you add? What are some desires or fears you are feeling after Unraveling or Severing?

BABY STEPS

As our hearts come back to life, they might hurt again. Many of us have closed ourselves off to God, Jesus, church, community, the Bible, or all kinds of other things. During the process of Rebuilding, we are going to feel things that touch upon past wounds. When I talk about opening a Bible again with a new viewpoint or checking out some kind of church service or spiritual discipline, you might feel afraid and tense up. Despite the weirdness, part of this season in our faith is being willing to take baby steps toward hope, trust, and trying again.

Popular Christian author and therapist Dan Allender wrote that when we start to move toward healing, hope, and new life, we might experience something like frozen memories. Initially we feel numb, but the pain really sets in when we start to slowly warm them up. As we thaw, we hurt. But it's a good ache because it means that blood is flowing where it had been cut off.[1]

Part of the struggle is sometimes feeling guilty. We may worry that others who are still Unraveling or haven't rebuilt anything will think we're being stupid, playing it too safe, or selling out. This can be extra tricky if we live with or are very close to someone who is still Unraveling. Some deconstructors wear a badge of honor that seems to say, "We picked it all apart, and we're a lot smarter than everyone else." I realize now how unfair that is. We each have our own experiences, and it's always best not to judge someone else's story.

Meg, who is slowly rekindling parts of her faith, shares that one of the hardest parts of her Unraveling was that she was still working on hers while others were already Rebuilding. It was hard for her not to feel resentful or left behind as others began to feel hope again. For a while everyone was changing at the same rate, questioning everything related to church and God. They had covert talks in coffee shops that they hoped no one overheard. When renewed faith emerges for some but not others, our struggles become more sensitive to talk about, even with good friends.

What happens when one friend is done with Jesus and another reembraces him? What happens when the Bible comes alive again for us but is still a deep source of angst for our dearest friend? I have felt this tension, feeling guilty for moving forward when others I know aren't yet sure where they will end up. My husband and I traveled a fairly similar time line together, although his faith shift was far less drastic than mine and he didn't carry the same ministry baggage.

Sometimes when others around us are Rebuilding and discovering firmer ground to stand on, we can feel sad, jealous, and even more off-kilter because we long for that too. Respect that feeling and your place in the process. Maybe you're not ready yet. Rebuilding can't be forced.

You may feel hesitant when Rebuilding because you fear being led back to conformity or blind affiliation. You buck under anything that might feel like an attempt to control you. For many, talking about a revived faith can feel like pressure to "come back to the Christian system" instead of a way to find a renewed spirituality. My whole purpose for writing *Faith Shift* is to provide a very loose framework for finding your way toward a new faith, not back to an old one.

If you're ready, consider moving away from the cynicism and skepticism of Unraveling and Severing toward what I call hopeful realism.

HOPEFUL BUT REALISTIC

Being cynical means being distrustful, critical, or pessimistic. Sound familiar? Do you feel any of these things as we start to talk about Rebuilding faith? Cynicism has its place in the faith-shifting process! Faking optimism isn't an option, playing nice would be false, and skipping over painful feelings would ruin us in the end. Melody Beattie, one of the premier voices on codependency and breaking free of unhealthy relationships, says, "If we don't feel our feelings and deal with them responsibly, they *will* control us."[2] Some people were openly distressed about my cynicism, having always associated me with positivity and hope. Looking back, though, I see its value as part of my healing. I'm also glad it hasn't prevailed.

Skepticism is related to cynicism. It can hinder us as we rebuild after Unraveling. It's true we need to approach issues of church and faith in a more discerning way. We can't get wowed, sucked in, shamed again. Yet, when we are always skeptical, we tend to notice the worst instead of the best. We're wary of trusting anyone and overreact. Although skepticism is more productive than cynicism, it's limiting and chokes off life. It creates a hardness of heart.

Remember Matt Damon's character in the film *Good Will Hunting*? Growing up in an abusive home and left to fend for himself, Will coped by shielding himself. His shell was so hard, though, that it didn't just protect him from getting hurt again; it also ensured that love couldn't enter. Cynicism and skepticism have a way of doing that to us.

Hopeful realism, on the other hand, is accepting things for what they are while being open to possibilities. When we are Rebuilding, our cynicism and skepticism will keep seeping in. We are not going to wake up tomorrow feeling free of them, so it's good to let go of that expectation. We may still feel triggered when we hear certain overtly spiritual words or end up in particular kinds of Christian conversations. Yet setting our intention on hopeful realism can radically lessen the impact. If hopeful realism is our filter, we will see what we encounter from a more honest perspective. When we engage with someone who is still happily living out a fused faith, we will honor their story instead of resent them for not understanding our situation. When we read something online about Christianity that starts to make our skin crawl, we will celebrate that we are in a different place.

Hopeful realism also helps us accept what we can't change and center our energies on what we can. It spurs us on to engage with our passion for justice and mercy in a tangible way by serving or volunteering with organizations we care about, Christian or not. We will take our eyes off the past and turn them toward the future. Instead of telling stories of where we've been, we will begin to tell stories of where we are trying to go. Cynicism and skepticism keep our hearts closed. Hopeful realism calls us to open our hearts in a new way.

As practitioners of hopeful realism, we'll discover what faith remains and learn that a little goes a long way. We'll find what works and be willing to engage with God in ways that might feel foreign but comforting. We will look back on our pasts not with disdain but with honor and respect. We'll celebrate the good things that were part of our story. Then we'll engage with our desire to serve, create, explore, and tangibly live out our passion for justice, mercy, and love in this broken world. We'll find ways to ignite these passions and courageously step into them despite how vulnerable we might feel. And yes, we'll process possibilities for community, connection, and even church and be willing to try new (or even old) experiences that draw us toward God, Jesus, and/or the Spirit and help us engage with others who care about the same things.

A LITTLE GOES A LONG WAY

But don't worry, you don't have to fling your heart open all at once. That's way too much to ask at this point. Most of us will have to rely on a less-dramatic start, a sliver of light, a streak of desire that pushes us out of the dark. We are ready for our dry bones to come back to life.

One of my favorite poems is by Cheryl Lawrie, a prison chaplain in Australia who writes beautiful, honest liturgies and understands faith shifts like few others. It's from Ezekiel 37:

you do not give up
on the broken and the lost

you do not give up
on the fractured
or the shattered
or the dying
or the dead

you do not give up
on the fearful
or the hateful
or the impossible

you do not give up
when there is no heartbeat left
or no heart at all

you do not give up
do not leave us for dead

thank god.[3]

Yes, thank God we are not left for dead. In Mary Karr's memoir *Lit*, her story of finding new life after a crippling alcohol addiction, she says,

If you live in the dark a long time and the sun comes out, you do not cross into it whistling. There's an initial uprush of relief at first, then—for me, anyway—a profound dislocation. My old assumptions about how the world works are buried, yet my new ones aren't yet operational. There's been a death of sorts, but without a few days in hell, no resurrection is possible.[4]

We've learned about loss in the Unraveling process. Our old assumptions about faith and life are buried, but our new ones haven't quite emerged yet. They can and will. As we walk through these Rebuilding chapters together, take good care of your heart.

Be honest about what you are thinking and feeling.

Go slowly.

Stay open.

Look for the light.

Know that hope exists.

Questions for Personal or Group Reflection

1. We're just beginning this journey of Rebuilding together, but how would you draw it on your own diagram?

2. On a scale from 1 to 10 (1 being not ready at all and 10 being very ready), how ready do you feel for Rebuilding? Describe why.

3. Look at the list on pages 129–130 of ways to know you're ready for Rebuilding. Which of these do you connect with? What would you add?

4. What scares you about engaging in some practices related to Rebuilding? What encourages you?

5. Consider these three possibilities on a continuum: *cynicism, skepticism,* and *hopeful realism.* Which of these resonate with you right now? Why?

6. Here's a challenging exercise to consider: Write down what you hope for in this next leg of the journey. What are you wishing for? What are you scared of? What are you open to? Try not to edit; just let your words flow onto the page.

11

Go Looking for What Remains

I no longer have to be what anyone else wants me to be. My faith and questions and God can be as big and bold as I want them to be. It is beautiful to have shed the chains of the old rules and just be.

—CHARITY

Often, as we travel this road of a renewed faith, we encounter fresh realizations that remind us we really are transforming. While I was working on this book, a young woman who was a part of the Refuge community died in a tragic alcohol-related accident. Christina was involved with our 12-Step group, and the accident was a devastating consequence of her relapse. It was a painful loss in countless ways, especially since I had been journeying with her for over nine years. Yet something interesting emerged in the midst of my grief. I recognized that although I was extremely angry at the realities of this broken world, at the ravages of addiction, at a beautiful life cut short, my feelings weren't directed at God and all the ways he may have allowed this to happen.

That's because several years ago, I let God off the hook. This simple but profound development was critical to rebuilding my faith. I still believe God is with us in the mess and that he cares about everything that happens to us, but I no longer espouse a theology where God is magically orchestrating every moment as part of a grand master plan. Do I think God is in all things, works in all things, and is in some weird way redeeming all things? Yes. But do I think God allowed that car accident to teach us some kind of cosmic lesson? No. Letting God off the hook has meant that I don't point the finger at God or try to pick apart "how we must have sinned" when things go wrong in the same way I used to. Recognizing that life this side of heaven is a bruised yet beautiful mess, and God's "Emmanuel-ness" is still true, has helped sustain me through a shifting faith. Yours are probably completely different, but we all have small and powerful truths that help us keep going.

Another interesting thing happened in the aftermath of my friend's death: I had to intersect with a traditional conservative church. Christina's parents attend a different church, and their leaders offered to have the memorial service at their facility. The only hitch was that they needed to confer with us as pastors to make sure we were in line theologically. On a conference call with one of their associate pastors, my friend and fellow pastor, Karl, and I were grilled on a long line of doctrinal questions. I felt a twisted pain in my gut and realized that if Karl hadn't been there, I would have been toast on several of the questions related to rigid doctrinal beliefs. A deeply angry feeling rose in the midst of it all.

A precious life had just been lost, and her family needed a place to celebrate her, so why in the world were these questions so important? After the conversation ended, the associate pastor called us back quickly to share that while we passed the theological test (no thanks to me, I'm sure), we couldn't hold the memorial service at their church if

I, as a female pastor, was part of officiating. That violated their view on women in leadership. My male co-pastor could speak from the pulpit, but I couldn't.

Yeah, it was an ugly moment, especially because I had been trying so hard to be kind and cooperative despite our theological differences. The good news is that the father immediately told him, "No thanks. There's no way we're doing this without Kathy, so we'll find another option." His response was extremely healing. But I will admit, the shame I felt in that moment, mixed with resentment against a church system that cares more about theological technicalities than about people's pain, caused a flood of emotions, making me yet again re-think what I believe and why. Later I thought about how Jesus would never have asked even one of those questions. The beliefs I still hold would be enough for him, but it's often not enough for others.

═══

One of the hardest things about my shift has been interacting with other believers who maintain a list of what is necessary to believe and do in order to fit their narrow definition of a Christian. It's also a primary reason so many people shed the descriptor of "Christian" when they deconstruct and reconstruct. I decided to hold on to the word in my effort to be part of redeeming it, but when people ask me if I am one, I usually say, "It depends on what you mean by *Christian*." When I look at the Gospels, I don't see a long list of beliefs the first followers needed to sign off on. Rather, I see Jesus calling the disciples to recognize their spiritual poverty and to move toward God with humility, willingness, desire, and openness. These attitudes are incredibly important to the season of Rebuilding. What we call ourselves isn't.

I still believe a few things about Jesus. It's not a long list. I am not saying that everyone's journey should look like mine. But for me, after everything else has been stripped away, I still believe Jesus is worth following. His compelling ways of embodying love, compassion, justice, and humility help me become a better person and the world a better place. No matter how much I value the teachings of other world religions or understand why people embrace atheism and humanism, I am still a Jesus-y person.

You may be way more into Jesus than I am, maybe you're not into him at all anymore, or maybe you are somewhere in between. But the questions are the same for all of us as we try to figure out life on the other side of a faith shift and discover what is left from our past that we can carry into the future.

DISCOVERING WHAT'S LEFT

The first part of engaging intentionally in the stage of Rebuilding is to consider this question: What do I still believe, even if it's just one small thing? Sometimes we think it's all gone, but if we dig we often discover remnants of our faith. Some parts are still alive and can't be taken away, no matter how hard we tried to shed them, or how much the systems we were part of tried to ruin them for us.

When I was working on my "Rebuilding After Deconstructing" blog series, I explored different doctrinal statements. I don't recommend that! It was a horribly disappointing, even angering, experience, and a reminder of how much of Christianity has been hijacked by "right belief" (as defined by whoever is writing the list). I believe Jesus came up with one statement that gives us plenty to work with for a lifetime: *Love God, love others as yourself* (see Matthew 22:37–39). I did not see one doctrinal statement that was as simple as Jesus's was, but I believe now, more than ever, that God doesn't have the same lists humans make. Anne Lamott says in her book *Plan B: Further Thoughts on Faith:* "I didn't need to understand the hypostatic unity of the Trinity; I just needed to turn my life over to whoever came up with redwood trees."[1]

As I mentioned, something that has sustained me is my belief that God is Emmanuel—he is with me, and he will never leave or forsake me. That has carried me through many a dark night. Many people shared their faith-shift experiences for this book. The range of responses to my question of "What remains?" varied. They said:

- God's grace—it's much bigger and more all-encompassing than I ever imagined or had been taught
- the need to love God, love others, love ourselves
- in more expansive ways, the theological concepts of repentance, redemption, and restoration
- the Apostles' and Nicene Creeds
- the existence of the Trinity—God, Jesus, and the Holy Spirit
- that God loves me just as I am
- "God is"
- that God loves all people
- that God is love, and the more I love, the more I participate in and am part of God
- the Bible calls me to love my neighbors
- the core value of community: life has to be lived with other people
- God is close to the brokenhearted
- love as expressed in 1 Corinthians 13
- Jesus's words that capsulize truths that still ring deep in my heart
- the gospel story of Jesus, and that he was sent to bring life, change, and hope to a world that was lost

- God is here, Jehovah Shammah
- God is good

I think that's a lovely list! For those of us who have unraveled, each remaining truth is a treasured gem. In many ways, the items on this list capture the simple essence of our faith, and I wonder if that was the big idea all along. Humans came along and made faith so complicated!

ONE THING STILL HOLDS

Years ago at our House of Refuge, a weekly gathering at our house with all kinds of faith shifters, the person facilitating asked us to think of one piece of faith we had held on to.

Our one thing looks radically different for each of us. Some of us may need much more to feel comfortable, but for others, realizing we have even one brings great hope. One thing is enough to sustain us as we navigate Rebuilding.

An important part of this step of discovering what remains is to remember that it's okay to still believe a lot of things that others have released. And, at the same time, it's also okay to let go of some of the things that others still believe passionately. If we start creating rules like "After Unraveling, we should be left with *A, B,* and *C*...or else," we are doing the same thing we are adamantly against. Each person's journey is unique. While I know some people who are no longer certain about the divinity of Jesus, others hold strongly to this belief. While some believe that the Bible might be inaccurate and therefore loses part of its authority, others still believe it is inerrant and take it extremely seriously. While some may have five or more things they still firmly believe, others may only have one.

The key is to allow ourselves the space to consider what is really left. What do I personally still believe? In 2006, a few of us from the founding leadership team wrote a statement for the Refuge to help others understand where we were coming from:

What We Believe (so far)
- Jesus meant everything he said.
- The Bible is our guiding text as Christ followers.
- In places, the Bible is hard to understand and even harder to apply.
- Believing is sometimes difficult.
- The more we learn of and experience God, the more questions we have.
- Miracles happen, sometimes quickly, but mostly they are slow in coming.
- We need each other in order to know God fully and live the life he dreams for us.
- It is our responsibility to advocate for and tangibly love the poor, marginalized, and oppressed.
- We value equality and dignity for all regardless of sex, race, socioeconomic status, or myriad other things that typically cause us to dominate others.
- We are embarrassed by how the word *Christian* is perceived in the world today and we are sorry for our part in that.
- Church is messy.

After all these years, even though I would make a few small changes, I can still basically espouse what's here. I like the "so far" in parentheses because it implies something critically important: *our faith is always evolving.* What I believe today, post-Unraveling and in the thick of Rebuilding, might still shift over time.

NOTICING WHAT IS MORE THAN WHAT ISN'T

As we move forward to a renewed faith, one of the most important principles we can embrace is that doubt is here to stay. After Unraveling, we can view doubt as an integrated extension of our lives. Years ago, a friend and I facilitated a Refuge conversation about doubt and faith by using several optical illusions. You know those pictures that show a face if you look at it from one side or an Eskimo going into an igloo if you saw it from another? Some saw one or the other right away, while a few saw both, or neither at all. What's always funny, though, is that in those moments some people in the group try to get others to see what they are seeing. "Can't you see that igloo?" they ask. "It's so obvious!"

It's that way with faith too. People can see the same God picture and view it completely differently. This is readily apparent in our Refuge community where we have a wide range of theological perspectives. As leaders, we have worked our tails off to create a space where people can hold differing beliefs. Some are definitely on the more conservative side while others would say they are deconstructing all they once believed. For some, the Bible feeds their souls. For others, it triggers weird feelings from past experiences. For some, worship fills a soul's longing, while for others the thought of singing words projected on a screen is the opposite of satisfying. For some, God feels real, close, intimate, kind, and good, while for others God is distant and harsh. It is incredibly tricky to live together in community under one big tent called Love. But we are learning how to respect that everyone might not see what we see, but it doesn't make us right and them wrong—or vice versa. The art of loving each other well is letting people be where they are and not trying to convince them to be where I am.

In our conversation about doubt and faith, we did a little exercise that helped people process this tension. We asked people to finish this sentence in two or three words:

Despite my doubt, I still believe _____.

The responses were gorgeous. The simplicity, the essence, the glory of something beautiful remaining after having so much stripped away was lovely to listen to, and I will always remember it.

I wish you and I could hang out in real life and talk about what remains for each of us in a few words. It would be so encouraging. Even though we can't, one thing we can do is share our stories with other men and women who have gone through Unraveling and are also Rebuilding their faith. My website, www.kathyescobar.com, has a "Faith Shifts" menu with some options for connecting and finding encouragement together.

Part of our personal work as Rebuilders requires excavating all of the rubble to find what remains, what is still part of our faith, no matter how big or small. Remember, people around us might not be able to handle this kind of stripping away, but God can. The question is, what are we going to do with it? Are we always going to spend energy on what we lost? (It definitely has its place, but over time we know that gets old.) Or are we going to center our attention on what is left? To let what remains sustain and guide us?

As we discover that something does indeed remain from our shredded faith, it frees us to consider what might help fan greater life into flame. Spiritual practices don't have to look the way they did in the past, and we can find what works to connect with God and our souls in simple and profound ways that tenderly rekindle our faith.

Questions for Personal or Group Reflection

1. Use these prompts as a way to start considering what remains.

    a) Even though I've unraveled so much, I do still believe

    _____.

    b) No matter what, my past experiences could never take away my _____.

    c) I still find hope in _____.

    d) Something I still trust about God, Jesus, the Holy Spirit, or all three is _____.

2. As you reflect on these, what is your "one thing," something that still remains no matter what?

3. Instead of writing *"What We Believe (so far),"* maybe we can capture *"What I Believe (for the moment)."* What would be on your list? Remember, it can be just one thing.

4. Do the things you believe right now provide any sustenance? Why or why not?

12

Finding What Works

*I stopped asking God to drop out of the sky to
come be with me and started opening up my
eyes to the reality he was already here.*

—ABBY

I met Maya after she e-mailed the Refuge, wondering if it might be a
safe place for her after she quit her job at a charismatic megachurch.
A gifted writer and recent college graduate who carried around a
heavy load of Christian baggage, Maya found her faith was fragile at
best. She did have a sincere desire to renew connection with God—
she just didn't know how anymore. After several meetings, it was
clear that what Maya needed from God was a sense of community:
people to look her in the eye, give her a hug, and remind her she wasn't
alone.

At first, showing up to Refuge gatherings wasn't an easy task for
her. But she dedicated herself to coming and sitting in the back during
our weekend service. Maya engaged with other people before and
after, even if it was just for a quick hug or hello. This helped her heart
open up again after being so shut down. She couldn't participate, sing,
or do any of the experiential exercises we offer during the service. But
she could show up and soak in some love for a few hours a week. She
kept asking me, "Are you sure it's okay that I don't participate?" I kept

reminding her that when it comes to faith, any possibility is worth pursuing if it brings hope and life.

⸺

I often say that Alcoholics Anonymous (AA) is the biggest underground church in the world. With no budgets, whiz-bang programming, or paid leadership, the raw and unplugged 12-Step meetings offer incredible transformation for men and women across ages and life experiences. While many churches spend millions of dollars unsuccessfully trying to create opportunities for healing and growth through complex ministry programs, AA offers life-changing, no-frills meetings for free. Although many dismiss the rich spirituality of the 12 Steps as "not Christian enough," the truth is that Jesus's ways are deeply embedded in all aspects of recovery.

Years ago a friend who leads local AA meetings facilitated our Wednesday House of Refuge gathering and said something I will never forget. When it comes to getting sober, Stephany shared, "People need to do whatever works for them as long as it doesn't harm or hurt anyone." Finding "whatever works" for addicts means discovering something that keeps them sober so that they can get more solid ground beneath their feet.

Finding "whatever works" for a Rebuilder means discovering anything that will help us open up our hearts to God again.

If you, like me, come from a conservative evangelical background, the thought of "whatever works" can conjure up trouble. We have been told to avoid anything that isn't firmly grounded in specific biblical truth (as interpreted by our leaders) or that contains even a scent of New Age spirituality (as defined by our leaders)—those who often have a sincere concern that anything "foreign" will lead us down a bad road and ultimately take us away from God.

I know this feeling well! Just the other night at the Refuge I closed our weekend gathering with a blessing. It was a poem by the Sufi poet Rumi, considered "dangerous" in my former circles, even though so much of his work is rooted in God's goodness and love. His poems always stir my soul, but after I shared, I experienced an annoying and painful flash of shame because I hadn't closed with a Bible verse instead. It felt nuts, honestly, after all these years of shifting in my faith, but it's a prime example of how deeply rooted messages from our pasts continue to rear their heads, trying to rob us of our ongoing freedom.

But the past can't win because finding what works is essential in our Rebuilding process. And when we miss God and long for connection again, any opening is better than none.

Finding what works is one of the cornerstones of rebuilding faith. It calls for effort, heart, and vulnerability, but it's worthwhile because it provides the sustenance we need to keep moving forward. When we are in a battle to reclaim our faith, we need to fan any flicker of spiritual connection into flame. When we're tired, hurting, and confused after unraveling what felt safe and familiar, we can't worry about spiritual technicalities and what others deem "valid" beliefs or practices. We can't focus on what other people might think of us. God is bigger than our former boxes and other people's boxes too.

Finding what works involves experimenting with practices that create life, passion, and connection. It's being willing to try spiritual practices we might have been afraid to try before or bravely reengaging with past disciplines. We must keep bridging the divide between the sacred and the secular and respect that God is always present—revealing, challenging, reminding, healing, inspiring, convicting, and loving. Instead of seeing things as spiritual only if they have a Bible verse, *God,* or *Jesus* attached to them, we can notice God's Spirit moving in our hearts through nature, music, people, work, and play. As we re-build, we can experiment with whatever works to make us feel alive, loved, and somehow connected to God and life.

You may wonder, *aren't we then just making God fit into what works for us? Isn't a spiritual life supposed to be about God, not us?* I always return to the example from Alcoholics Anonymous. Over time, those in recovery will have to do all kinds of other hard things and participate in uncomfortable practices of making amends, extending forgiveness, and changing habits. For people who are renewing faith, whatever works now won't work forever. Over time, we will need to engage in different practices we don't like or that feel extremely un-pleasant in order to grow. But not right now, when our tender faith is this fragile and vulnerable. We need some solid experiences under our belts first to strengthen us for our future.

THE ART OF EXPERIMENTING SPIRITUALLY

When we are coming out of Unraveling (and maybe Severing) and Rebuilding our tender faith, we need to go slowly. It may take a long time for our hearts to reopen to God and others. Some of our legalistic spiritual practices almost ruined us, so we can't expect them to bring us life today. I remember trying to reengage with the Bible after a long period of not being able to read it without getting angry. I tried all of my former habits: randomly opening it and seeing where I landed, reading the Gospels straight through, processing one psalm at a time, and journaling about what I read. Everything fell flat. My old church leaders had taken so much out of context and distorted it that my old filters just got in the way. The harder I tried to force myself to "get it" in the same way I used to, the worse I felt. It's when I gave up trying to make the old ways fit the new me that fresh avenues began to make my heart feel more alive.

I admit, I felt guilty about it at first: *What is wrong with me?! Why can't I get any of those old feelings back?* But now, in hindsight, I wish someone had told me that measuring my faith against the past would only make matters worse. I had to throw out the old maps about spiritual practices and stop seeking a spiritual high. I needed to do whatever I could to nurture my fledgling faith.

Recently, Nicole, a young mom and working professional, hit a brick wall in her faith. She had been slowly Unraveling, but something radically shifted when she recognized the painful realities of patriarchy in the church and the awful tilt against women around the world. Rage against a male, dominating God whom she had been taught to blindly follow began to rise as she got in touch with her own story of sexual violations. Part of Nicole's finding "what works" is allowing herself to dive into the deep end and explore the feminine side of God. It has felt heretical and blasphemous after a lifetime of viewing God only as masculine, but she is pushing through her fear and finding life through the feminine Divine. Nicole is scared for some people to know because she's sure they will blast her with scriptures and lengthy judgments. And she wonders if she is violating some unwritten code that says God will be with us only if we view him/her a certain way. I told my friend, "If this is helping you find life, energy, and challenge in your faith, go with it. God is in the process. Keep finding what works. It's the hard work of Rebuilding."

Here are some possible practices or questions to help you experiment productively during this season of Rebuilding:

- What makes you feel alive? What makes you feel loved? What are you passionate about?

- Explore different ways to connect with God that your previous faith tradition might not have validated, such as nature, social activism, contemplative practices, and so on. (We'll explore this more intentionally in the pages that follow.)

- If reading the Bible feels freaky right now, put it on the shelf and find something else to read that is inspiring and challenging. Many other faith traditions have amazing material worth bravely exploring.

- If you miss the Bible and want to try it again, practice reading it for its beauty and inspiration instead of for study or knowledge.

- If connecting with God as Father is disconcerting, consider another aspect of God's character and image that brings life. As a spiritual director, I often ask people, "What part of God do you want to connect with, or do you really need, right now?" Start there. It could be God as Friend, Jesus, Holy Spirit, Mother, Creator, Advocate, and so on.

- Practice soul care by doing whatever revives you. Go to a movie, read a book, make music, or just rest. Whenever our souls are strengthened, God is in the midst.

- Create something. Art comes in many different forms, but most people feel more alive and connected to their souls when they participate. Write, draw, paint, build, make a collage, or take pictures.

- If you're still attending church, go to the social hour and visit with people you love but then leave when the leadership starts preaching, singing, or whatever might cause a painful reaction. Let yourself reject what you need to.

- Have some fun. Sometimes we take ourselves—and our faith journeys—far too seriously. Clearly they're important, but it's good to lighten our load sometimes through laughter and joyful activity. It makes me think of Anne Lamott and the simple wisdom her friend once left her on an answering machine: "The road to enlightenment is long and difficult, and you should try to not forget snacks and magazines."[1]

WHAT'S WORKED FOR OTHERS

One of the most sustaining pieces of my faith journey has been sticking with what makes my heart come alive: people. Community, connection, and conversations have kept me somehow tethered to God. People—not worship songs or reading the Bible or nature—keep faith at work. I resonate deeply with what Rhoda Janzen wrote in her book *Mennonite in a Little Black Dress:* "When you're young, faith is often a matter of rules. What you should do and shouldn't do, that kind of thing. But as you get older, you realize that faith is really a matter of relationship—with God, with the people around you, with the members of your community."[2]

Many of my friends started creating art during their faith shift and have found it to be the most spiritually nourishing thing that's ever happened to them. Throwing clay on a wheel, taking a painting class, learning photography, dancing, or writing poetry, stories, or blogs can be profound spiritual practices. Moving our bodies through yoga, martial arts, or sports can open up our souls to God in new and wonderful ways. Others are finding life through Orthodox, Episcopal, or Catholic liturgical practices, exploring faith in ways that are completely different from those they grew up with.

Sometimes loving and serving others is what works. In her delightful memoir *Take This Bread,* Sara Miles reflects on how she didn't know any of the rules of Christianity when she intersected with God's Spirit through communion at an Episcopal church in San Francisco. She just knew something happened in her soul, and it led her to start a food pantry. She connected with God through providing food for others. She writes:

> Faith working through love...could mean plugging away with other people, acting in small ways without the comfort of a big vision or even a lot of realistic hope. It could look more like prayer: opening yourself to uncertainty, accepting your lack of control. It meant taking on concrete tasks in the middle of confusion, without stopping to argue about who was the truest believer. Whatever else, I could at least keep working in the pantry, feeding as many people as I could.[3]

Each of us has a different thing that works for us, but the key in Rebuilding is to explore possibilities and nurture any that help lighten our souls. As we do, we'll build beautiful bridges to God over time.

DIFFERENT WAYS OF LOVING GOD

One of the most overused phrases in all of Christianity is *We just need to love God.* What does that mean? In many of the contexts we unraveled from, it has completely different definitions. For evangelicals, loving God comes through appreciation of the Bible, sharing Jesus with others, and expressing our need for Christ's atonement because of our humanness. Those from a more charismatic tradition are taught that loving God means inspirational worship and prayer experiences. For Catholics, loving God is about honoring his holiness through Mass and Confession. For Mormons, loving God is often focused on serving the church faithfully with obedience. Many from mainline denominations love God through attending church and serving the community.

These are generalizations, of course, and you could plug in all kinds of different ideas for what loving God meant in your former faith. The point is that these definitions are really limiting. A few weeks ago at the Refuge, Karl shared that the Scriptures were summed up with "Love God." He said, "The problem is that I don't know what love is, and I am not sure who God is...but other than that I've got it nailed down." We all laughed, because we know it's true. As we rebuild our faith after Unraveling, we discover many more ways to love, connect, commune, or hang out with God than we had ever been taught.

In his book, *Sacred Pathways: Discover Your Soul's Path to God,* Gary Thomas challenges readers to consider various ways to commune with God.[4] He shares that there are nine different pathways to spiritual connection. When we modified some of this material for an experience at the Refuge, we added a tenth one. The ways include loving God through

1. Nature
2. Our senses
3. Ritual and liturgy
4. Silence and solitude
5. Activism
6. Caring for others
7. Mystery and celebration
8. Contemplation
9. Our minds
10. Recovery

As you search for what works, review these ten ways of connecting with God. Skip ones that don't describe you or are representative of the faith system you left behind. Don't let what doesn't work trip you up and instead focus on what does or what might. Remember that all of these are possibilities for us, but as Gary Thomas fleshes out in his book, some will resonate more naturally.

1. *Naturalists* connect with God through nature. They learn the best God lessons in the outdoors, where we can visualize scriptural truths, see God more clearly, and learn to rest. Naturalists feel free and unconstricted when they are outside.

2. *Sensates* connect with God through the senses. They see God in art or when they feel textures, listen to music, smell perfume, or taste food.

3. *Traditionalists* connect with God through ritual and symbol. They value iconic symbols and liturgical practices. They appreciate reading or saying specific prayers and place a high value on the beauty of the church calendar, including the practices of Lent and Advent.

4. *Ascetics* love God through silence and solitude. They love being alone with God and value simplicity. They make room for quiet and value fasting and praying.

5. *Activists* connect with God through confrontation and social justice. They are spiritually nourished through the battle for a cause, and they connect with God through advocating on behalf of others. They offer time and energy to create change.

6. *Caregivers* connect with God through loving others. They love to care for others in a variety of ways, including listening, actively helping, and repairing broken things for

others. They feel close to God when they are engaged with other people.

7. *Enthusiasts* connect with God through mystery and celebration. They love getting caught up in worship experiences and look for movements of God—both big and small—in every interaction. They are expectant about God's power and possibility and are fueled by dreams and visions.

8. *Contemplatives* connect with God through adoration and resting in God's presence. They value spending time with God through different forms of prayer and meditation. Using labyrinth walks, reflective stations, and quiet retreats fills their souls.

9. *Intellectuals* connect with God through the mind. They love the Bible, systematic theology, and creeds. They value beliefs about God and are stimulated by Bible studies, lectionaries, and historical texts as well as philosophical conversations about God.

10. *Healers* connect with God through recovery. They feel close to God when they are powerless and desperate. They experience connection with God through the principles of the 12 Steps and find God's love through acknowledging their own and others' pain.

Which of these do you relate to? As you read through the descriptions, did you notice any strong feelings about particular ones? Were any negatively or positively connected to your former church experiences?

This list validates a much wider spectrum of spiritual connection than many of us were taught. Part of Rebuilding is appreciating our uniqueness (maybe for the first time) and embracing the freedom to be

who we are (and to let others be who they are too). Most church systems are built on a central path; people inside the system receive a
message that "This is *the* way" to connect with God. When we aren't
wired the same way or we've shifted, such rules can really mess with
our heads.

One of the most freeing parts of this exercise was recognizing that
my top three ways are connecting with God through caregiving, activism, and healing. My history was with churches where Intellectuals
and Enthusiasts were most highly valued; their practices counted as
"godly" and "spiritually correct." They appeared to exemplify the core
of "mature Christianity." Part of the catalyst for my Unraveling was
feeling unvalued for caring about people more than Bible studies and
feeling less spiritual than others because I didn't use certain language.

We can still learn and grow from practices we are less drawn to.
Of course, it's good to stretch and expand. But as we open ourselves up
to renewing connection with God after a faith shift, we can use this
framework to find what helps us come more alive right now. Don't
evaluate what works now against the past or what your friend or partner might be more interested in. Honor your own uniqueness and
allow yourself to own it.

REENGAGING WITH SCRIPTURE
(A GUIDE FOR THE ALLERGIC)

Many of us have a broken relationship with the Bible because of the
ways our former faith systems twisted and tainted it. It's supposed to
be a source of life, hope, goodness, and love, but for all kinds of reasons
many of us have become sort of allergic to it, especially if in our past
people used it as a weapon.

I often tell people in major faith shifts that if the Bible (or a certain Christian author's work) is too toxic, take a break from it. A healthy separation (just as when a marriage is in trouble) can provide room for healing. Many fear that a separation will lead to a divorce, but in pastoral counseling I've often seen it's just the opposite. Time and intentional space away can prepare the way for restoration in the end.

What happens, however, when we are transitioning and feel a stirring to reengage with the Bible? Following are some answers, but this section isn't for everyone. You may need to keep your Bible on the shelf for now to preserve your soul as you heal. These ideas are for you if you think it's time to give the Bible a try again. As with everything else in this book, take what you need and leave the rest.

- Meditate on one passage you really like for a while. You don't have to study, exegete, explain, justify, or know the Greek words for it to do something in your heart.

- Look up that same passage in different Bible versions that you might have been expected to avoid before (www.Bible gateway.com has numerous translations worth experimenting with).

- Practice *Lectio Divina,* also known as "Divine Reading," which replaces studying the Bible with intersecting emotionally with the passage. Read the passage several times and notice words, feelings, or soul stirrings. Some passages worth considering for faith shifters—because they're less likely to trip sensitive theological wires—are: Psalm 23; Psalm 40:1–3; Isaiah 43:1–4; Isaiah 61:1–4; Matthew 5:3–10; Colossians 3:12–15; Ephesians 3:14–19; Luke 15:11–32.

- Read a passage and then rewrite it in your own words.

- After reading one of Jesus's parables or a different passage, ask
  yourself these questions. Journal your answers, if you like:

   What is a different title for it?

   What does it tell me about the tendencies of human
   beings?

   What does it tell me about my own heart and life?

   This passage makes me feel…

   Originally, I was taught that this passage meant…

   I wonder if it could actually mean…

   Today, it makes me consider…

   How does this point me toward loving God more?

   loving others more? loving myself more?

- Read a psalm and then write your own. Here are some
  prompts that can guide you:

   God, I am feeling really…

   Right now, life is…

   I long for you to…

   I am wondering why…

   I am trying to remember that…

   I am thankful for…

- Read the passage as if it were being read to a community
  of people, not just to you. What does it call people to, as a
  group?

- Try reading just the red print, the words of Jesus, if your
  Bible has this feature.

- Read the passage through the eyes of the child. What do
  you see or hear?

What would you add? Some of these questions work not only for
biblical texts, but for other inspirational books as well.

LIVING INTO THE POSSIBILITIES

Experimenting with possibilities beyond our former experience, find-ing ways we uniquely connect with God, and possibly reengaging with the Bible are all pieces of Rebuilding our faith. As with other aspects of a faith shift, this is a messy, experimental process, and we sometimes have to try things that don't work to find things that do. Be brave. Don't listen to the voice that tells you that you are a heretic for reading certain books, trying particular practices, or exploring new avenues of spirituality.

As you find what works, be gentle with yourself (and maybe with God too). Be careful of feeling shame when you don't feel connected in the way you want to. And don't let yourself be shamed by others who say, "You are doing *what?!*" Try not to conclude that there's something wrong with you, and instead trust that healing some of your faith allergies may take a long time. Many avenues for commun-ing with God exist and are worth searching for as you find what works in Rebuilding.

As we close this chapter, consider the words of the Rumi poem I mentioned previously. May they sink in and challenge you to risk your heart and keep finding what works.

> Today, like every other day, we wake up empty and frightened.
> Don't open the door to the study and begin reading.
> Take down a musical instrument.
> Let the beauty we love be what we do.
> There are hundreds of ways to kneel and kiss the ground.[5]

There are hundreds of ways to connect with God. As we spark new hope and connection with him, we can gain the strength and courage to look at our past with new eyes. We can celebrate the good that existed in our old faith as we keep opening ourselves to embrace the new.

Questions for Personal or Group Reflection

1. What makes your heart feel more alive right now? What brings passion or life? (Remember, it doesn't have to be on a list of what is supposedly spiritual.)

2. Consider the ten different ways to connect with God. Which resonated most for you? Which ones made you feel uncomfortable because you used to do them or felt as if you were supposed to? Which would you like to explore more right now?

3. How can you build more of these specific practices into your life? What others would you add to the list? What are some steps you might take to nurture them in a tangible way?

4. How do you feel about reengaging with the Bible? As you read through the ideas to try, are there any worth considering right now?

5. What's working for you right now when it comes to connecting with God? Remember, it can be one thing or it can be a longer list. Sharing your experience with others can be helpful as they are exploring new options too.

Honoring the Good in What Was

There's no going back to the past
for me, but without its legacy
there'd be no going forward, either.

—Edward

When I noticed an old picture at my in-laws' house of Jose and me with our three oldest kids dressed in their BabyGap best, I flashed back. In our "good Christian" days, we were trying to keep up with what the contemporary church required of us as a young, put-together family. We were staunchly conservative Bible study leaders, dedicated to protecting our children from the ravages of public school. At that point we possessed not even a sliver of understanding of why someone wouldn't want to be part of church. That world feels so far away from where we live now.

It would be easy to look at our smiles then as painted on or to assume that that season wasn't authentic. But the truth is our faith was genuine. A powerful period in our spiritual journey, those years shaped us in crucial, life-changing ways. The pictures we took captured that time and space, but now what's behind our smiling eyes is completely different.

As we continue to move toward greater hope and freedom in our faith as part of Rebuilding, it's important not to reject or remain bitter about the past. Healing can come as we find ways to *celebrate what was* as a way to move toward the future. Some things about our past experiences are worthy of respect and honor. There are ideas, events, and/or people we can celebrate for forming who we are today. Celebrating what was isn't about looking at the past through rose-colored glasses, creating false memories to feel better, or forcing ourselves to go where we can't emotionally go. Rather, it's about remembering that what we left behind is a significant part of our unfolding story.

This idea of celebrating or honoring is often missing from conversations during deconstructing and Unraveling. We can share so much angst, anger, and harshness about what was wrong with our faith and church experiences that we forget that some things—many, actually—were right about them too. Some of us have more good memories or substance than others to celebrate, but this practice can be incredibly restorative as we move beyond Unraveling and further into Rebuilding.

FOR THOSE RECOVERING FROM SPIRITUAL ABUSE

Some of us have been victims of spiritual abuse at the hands of specific leaders and destructive systems. I am absolutely not asking you to find the good in a system that hurt you emotionally, spiritually, and possibly physically. That would be harmful and counterproductive to your healing. But I challenge you to consider whether anything good related to God came out of that season. In so many abusive systems, God and humanity become so tangled up it's hard to decipher what's what, but many people, after a lot of personal work, are able to see the goodness, faithfulness, and unconditional love of God through the darkness of harmful systems.

This is not true for everyone, however, so don't try to conjure up anything. Don't feel guilty for not being able to celebrate a darn thing when it comes to your abusive past. You get an honorable pass from this exercise. Your soul has been through a great storm, and the best way to keep moving forward is to respect the truth of your past instead of trying to celebrate anything about it.

If you're not ready, don't feel pressure to work through this chapter right now. Listen to your heart and be mindful of how you are feeling. This is your journey. As you read through the sections that follow, take good care of your soul. Pay special attention to your internal radar on what you can and can't handle moving forward.

"FIND THE GOOD AND PRAISE IT"

For those of us who didn't suffer from overtly abusive systems but rather came from run-of-the-mill dysfunctional churches and ministries, it's a worthy exercise to consider what good came from our past. Alex Haley, the author of the famous slave epic, *Roots,* says, "Find the good, and praise it."[1] When it comes to finding our way forward in our faith, this simple yet powerful kernel of wisdom goes a long way.

June, a steadfast advocate for refugees relocating to Denver from countries around the globe, was raised in an impoverished, rural community where life revolved around church family. Her church was very conservative and rigid, and her Rebuilding story has involved extracting a long list of negative messages. Yet, as she sorted through the baggage of her early faith experience, she found some gems. Bedrock values such as "People are more important than things" and "Share what you have" have sustained her. Also, because June's church was like family, the depth of their connection through the years "helps me now to have grace for people who are ideologically opposite me. I know their stories, and I know many have deeply generous and sincere spirits. So there's love among them, even if we don't have much common ground." June is learning to honor the good from the past and leave the rest behind.

So am I. Instead of rejecting where I've been and being mad at myself for some of the things I believed and the ways I behaved, I am learning to celebrate the past as part of my ongoing spiritual and emotional development. Here are some things I'm learning to honor from my past. As you read through my list, consider what you might want to celebrate from yours:

- Almost all of the scriptures that I know and love are ones I learned during those early times of intense learning and study.

- I came from a broken home with very little structure, and even though I reject the rigidity of my old church's rules now, having a clear, guiding framework for living was helpful in my early adult years.

- Gathering regularly with other people to talk about our faith instilled a deep desire for intention and community that still motivates me today.

- Coming from an unstable home life, I found the comfort and security of being part of a family who believed and did the same things was very healing.

- I made a lot of amazing friends. Some think I've gone off the deep end, but many others still love me, and we remain connected despite differing practices and beliefs.

- Though some of our Christian parenting practices weren't healthy, we still gained helpful tools related to grace and character development that we use today in our parenting.
- During those years, the wow factor drew me in, stirred my soul, and made me want to connect with God. Even though it wore out its welcome, it had its place.

You might look at this list and scoff, "Um, that's it? That's all that came out of those years of Fusing?" But for me, these beautiful kernels of good stir up respect and gratitude.

Samuel, an outspoken retired government employee who has since become his neighborhood's ad hoc chaplain, completely unraveled his connection to organized religion. But today he remains committed to serving the homeless and has become passionate for the LGBT community in his city. Often he has nothing good to say about past church systems. He saw too many unhealthy things. Samuel's faith in God never left, but his faith in the system dissolved completely. Celebrating the past wasn't his favorite exercise, but as he explored it, he admitted that one good thing did come from the church: people. Samuel has a deep gratitude for the people he met along the way. That's the only thing he wants to linger from his church past, and that is enough.

Celebrating what was makes us vulnerable; it is much easier to keep our hearts protected, hardened, and focused on the negative. Remembering the good is riskier, but so much healthier too. In her call for us to live a more courageous, wholehearted life, Barbara Brown Taylor recommends the practice of gratitude.

To become fully human means learning to turn my gratitude for being alive into some concrete common good. It means growing gentler toward human weakness. It means practicing forgiveness of my and everyone else's hourly failures to live up to divine standards…. It means receiving the human condition as blessing not curse, in all its achingly frail and redemptive reality.[2]

I would add "and the church's hourly failures to live up to divine standards" as well. Sure, it might be hard to thank the past, but it's a reminder that we are flawed humans who are part of flawed human systems.

Redemption and healing can come, but we've got to look for it and be brave enough to be grateful for it. That's how beauty comes from ashes.

EMBRACING PARADOX

Father Richard Rohr writes, "A paradox is something that appears to be a contradiction, but from another perspective is not a contradiction at all. You and I are living paradoxes, and therefore most prepared to see ourselves in all our reality. If you can hold and forgive the contradictions within yourself, you can normally do it everywhere else, too."[3]

Rohr challenges me to break out of immature and dualistic thinking that is centered on either/or when it comes to faith. In the spiritual constructs I come from, things were either all good or all bad. You were either a true believer or one of the lost, a Bible-centered person or a liberal-anything-goes person, a prideful self-centered person or a faithful godly one. These extremes created an incredible split in me, especially because I could never measure up to the "good" ones. The stage of Fusing focuses on *either/or* thinking while Rebuilding is built upon *both/and*: we can struggle with Believing and also have faith; we can love/value the Bible and still vote for a Democrat; we can have both self-centeredness and humility in us at the same time. We can bravely seek deeper connection with God and be afraid of it.

The late Brennan Manning, a Catholic priest who spent his life sharing the message of God's grace, wrote,

> When I get honest, I admit I am a bundle of paradoxes. I believe and I doubt, I hope and get discouraged, I love and I hate, I feel bad about feeling good, I feel guilty about not feeling guilty. I am trusting and suspicious. I am honest and I still play games. Aristotle said I am a rational animal; I say I am an angel with an incredible capacity for beer.[4]

Embracing paradox is one of the most helpful tools I've gleaned in this messy faith-shifting process. I can feel confused and hopeful at the same time, sad and happy, vulnerable and strong, unsettled and peaceful, disconnected and somehow strangely connected. I can also feel frustrated with and confused about God but remain simultaneously drawn toward him too.

Faith is both clear and fuzzy, simple and complicated, freeing and confusing. Fact is, all the craziness of our past can live in harmony with all the craziness of our present and future. We all do better when we allow the good and bad, dark and light, past and present to live together. Much freedom can come as we better learn how to embrace the paradoxes in ourselves and our stories. As we do that, it's far more likely we can accept them in other people, systems (as in churches and organizations), and God as well.

In other words, if I can't see myself as a paradox—both flawed and whole, weak and strong—I can't see others (or God or the church or the Bible) as paradoxes, either. This is no easy task, as my natural tendency is to try to squeeze out anything negative so that only the good remains. The trouble is that never happens, and I lose a lot of living in the present along the way. Rebuilding faith requires acknowledging paradox. It opens up our view of God instead of limiting it to only what feels acceptable from our past experiences.

As we celebrate what was, it's good to reflect on the paradoxes of our past. For example, when I look at my season of Fusing, I see how it was rigid—filled with a narrow view of God and acceptable beliefs and behaviors—but also full of healing and hope. When I think about where I am with God today, I see my faith as sensitive and strong— sensitive because many things still touch the open nerves of a faith shift, but strong because it has endured the stripping away of so much.

Think about this in regard to your own life. What was the paradox of your faith prior to Shifting? What two contradicting words describe it? Now, consider where you are at the moment. What two words describe your faith today?

Celebrate these! It reminds us that in the midst of the bad, there's always good.

A TIME TO...

Ecclesiastes 3:1–8 captures the essence of honoring what was.

For everything there is a season, a time for every activity under heaven.

A time to be born and a time to die.
A time to plant and a time to harvest.
A time to kill and a time to heal.
A time to tear down and a time to build up.
A time to cry and a time to laugh.

A time to grieve and a time to dance.

A time to scatter stones and a time to gather stones.

A time to embrace and a time to turn away.

A time to search and a time to quit searching.

A time to keep and a time to throw away.

A time to tear and a time to mend.

A time to be quiet and a time to speak.

A time to love and a time to hate.

A time for war and a time for peace.

Acknowledging and celebrating what was helps us leave it behind and embrace what is now. I wrote my own version of Ecclesiastes 3 several years ago as a reminder that the past has its place and time, but the present is where we want to live now.

For everything there is a season, a time for every activity under heaven.

A time for quiet strength to be born, and a time for insecurity to die.

A time to plant courage, and a time to harvest peace.

A time to kill self-hatred, and a time to heal from fear of abandonment.

A time to tear down walls that protect me, and a time to build up hearts that love me.

A time to cry about how hard it's been, and a time to laugh about how hard it's been.

A time to grieve over the loss of my once-certain faith, and a time to dance because my soul is coming back to life.

A time to scatter people who can't handle me being me, and a
time to gather people who can.

A time to embrace my voice, and a time to turn away
from worrying about what other people think.

A time to search for balance, and a time to quit searching for
the finish line.

A time to keep what's important, and a time to throw
away all the rest.

A time to tear apart "right doctrine," and a time to mend what
I deeply believe.

A time to be quiet about what isn't, and a time to speak
about what is.

A time to love slow and steady transformation in myself and
others, and a time to hate impatience.

A time for war against resistance, and a time for peace in
the chaos.

Amen.

As we keep traveling forward on this bumpy, beautiful road looking for signs of life, we turn our attention to the passions we have inside of us to love, serve, create, advocate, and cultivate some of our dreams. The next part of Rebuilding is finding ways to ignite these passions.

Questions for Personal or Group Reflection

1. On a scale of 1 to 10 (with 1 being easy and 10 being hard), what number describes how you feel about celebrating or honoring what used to be part of your faith? Why?

2. Each person's list of what to celebrate looks different. Take the time and consider some good that came from your years in Fusing. When you're ready, write down whatever comes to mind.

3. If you want to try a different angle on this, start a gratitude list when it comes to the past. What are you grateful for about your pre-unraveled faith?

4. What do you think about paradox—embracing two contradicting things at the same time—when it comes to faith? How would acknowledging the paradoxes of the past and present help you move forward? Think of two contradicting words that describe your years of Fusing. Now think of two words that describe where you are now, after Unraveling. If you need a little help getting started, here are some lists:

Dark: ambivalent, angry, apprehensive, bound, broken, bumpy, challenging, closed, confusing, dark, dead, depressing, empty, exhausting, fierce, frustrating, hard, heavy, insecure, irritating, lonely, messy, scary, scattered, shattered, tired, turbulent, ugly, unnerved, unsettled, vulnerable, weak, weary

Light: abundant, alive, awake, beautiful, compassionate, connected, creative, curious, delighted, easy, empowered, encouraging, free, fulfilled, full, genuine, glorious, grateful, light, loud, noble, open, pretty, proud, quiet, redeemed, restored, revived, rich, safe, satisfied, secure, smooth, strong, whole

5. Here is a template you can use to create your own "A Time to…" piece that helps celebrate both the past and the present.

For everything there is a season, a time for every activity under heaven.

A time for _____ to be born and a time for _____ to die.

A time to plant _____ and a time to harvest _____.

A time to kill _____ and a time to heal from _____.

A time to tear down _____ and a time to build up _____.

A time to cry about _____ and a time to laugh at _____.

A time to grieve over _____ and a time to dance because _____.

A time to scatter _____ and a time to gather _____.

A time to embrace _____ and a time to turn away from _____.

A time to search for _____ and a time to quit searching for _____.

A time to keep _____ and a time to
throw away _____.

A time to tear apart _____ and a time to
mend _____.

A time to be quiet about _____ and a
time to speak about _____.

A time to love _____ and a time to hate
_____.

A time for war against _____ and a time
for peace in _____.

Becoming More Alive

Passions are dangerous, but as I talk about
them, I feel a spark of life in my soul.
—KATHERINE

Daniel worked as a manager for a large telecommunications company. A steady job with a solid income and benefits, it was a good fit for his scientific mind and organizational skills. It also provided flexibility to offer his gifts to the local church for many years, and he was heavily invested in serving and leading worship. After experiencing one too many church splits, Daniel found his passion for the church crumbling. He began listening to his heart more carefully. It was crying out for a more meaningful profession and a way to use his gifts outside of the church. He decided to use his last few years before retirement to go to graduate school part-time and pursue a degree in counseling. Each semester, he began to feel his deadened heart come back to life and now he is thriving in his own private practice. Watching his transformation is beautiful to see.

I keep discovering that I can't think or study my way into a new life. No book, retreat, or conference will make it all better. Trust me, if it existed, I would have found it already. My only hope moving forward is to *live my way into a new life.* Renewed living requires investigating our passions and finding ways to act on them. We all have dreams—things we'd like to do, build, try, or be part of. These can be big or small, exciting or simple, things related to church or not at all spiritual. Regardless of the size or type, part of Rebuilding is acknowledging our desires to pursue some of these things. St. Irenaeus said, "The glory of God is man fully alive."[1]

To me, igniting passions is about specific ways of serving, loving, creating, and living. These words, often attributed to the Sufi poet Hafiz, say it beautifully: "An awake heart is like a sky that pours light."

Many of us have been told that passions, hopes, and dreams are selfish unless they directly benefit the church. We've heard we aren't supposed to enjoy what we are doing but rather serve for the sake of God. Another message is that because of our gender or abilities, we aren't allowed or qualified to do certain things. Hear me on this: these are lies! God's image is best reflected in men and women fully alive. A world in need of our gifts lies far beyond the walls of the church. In fact, the world would be a much better place if the church unleashed its people to freely serve and love in all kinds of wild contexts that leadership has no control over.

Years ago, a friend challenged me, saying, "It's okay to do something just because you want to do it." It sounds silly to people outside the church, but those of us who have weird, distorted God messages find them obstacles to our passions. It's okay to do things because we like them, not because we think God does or other people think we should. Over time, I realized that I pastor the Refuge because I am crazy about people, messes, and transformation. Sure, I believe God is in the midst of it, but I am not afraid to say that I do this work because I like it, not because God is telling me I have to. The shift from obligation to owning and pursuing a heart's desire can be transformational.

ESCAPING THE OLD IMPOSSIBILITIES

Let's look at the some of the distorted messages we've received about our passions.

1. "It's Not Allowed"

Katherine, a woman with deep brown eyes and a shy smile, is a gifted writer who bravely shared with a family member her dream of writing a science-fiction novel. She then faced a long list of reasons why that genre was not consistent with her Christian faith. The harsh reality of her family member's response magnified the voice inside her that said, *You're not allowed to do, want, or try certain things.* Not everyone has this dilemma, but it's impossible to ignite our passions without addressing the subtle or direct negative messages that block our movement. We may have to accept that some of our friends and family may never understand, and we have to do what we need to do anyway. As Eleanor Roosevelt famously said, "You must do the thing which you think you cannot do."[2]

2. "You're Not Qualified"

Another obstacle to fulfilling our passions is feeling as if we are not talented enough or qualified to manage it. It is a primary reason people remain hunkered in the shadows, afraid to move forward. We don't want to be perceived as haughty. My friend Samantha is an extremely talented therapist, yet sometimes she doubts her gifts after years of being in a controlling church environment where every motive was scrutinized. She still struggles with "wanting" anything because that was perceived as pride, and therefore sinful, in her previous circle. Recently, when I was talking to her about expanding her practice, she immediately began reciting the long list of reasons she wasn't qualified. Later, she called me and shared that she realized her resistance was from being afraid to step into more.

3. "As a Woman [Man], You Can't Do That"

Christian women have an extra measure of shame related to wanting to do and be more. Brené Brown says, "The issue of 'stay small, sweet, quiet and modest' sounds like an outdated problem, but the truth is that women still run into those demands whenever we find and use our voices."[3] Many women are healing from faith experiences where they weren't valued equally to men. Considered "less than," we weren't allowed to lead or serve freely alongside our male counterparts.

Paula has a master's in divinity from an acclaimed seminary and is a gifted leader. She tried and tried to make her gifts work in multiple church systems. Filled with passion for community development and collaboration, she kept bumping up against the same old prejudices everywhere she turned. She was valued for how she could serve a particular church but not for her passion for the wider one.

At first, Paula settled for anything she could get, but as her strength increased, she knew, "I have to find somewhere I can freely live out who I am called to be." We are grateful that spot was the Refuge, and it's awesome to see her fulfill her dreams and start to flourish. It's been slow, though, and we still have a long way to go until she feels fully empowered and supported. She offers, "I'm excited about the possibilities here, but I also feel really extremely vulnerable, not knowing if I am going to overstep my bounds or be misperceived as 'too much' by others."

Many women conclude that the only way to freely use their gifts is to leave the church completely. They have built businesses, written books, gone back to school, and found success in the secular world. Bottom line: women often find themselves up against an extra measure of resistance that can cause them to retreat or doubt their abilities.

But men also have trouble trying new things when they aren't "practical." Many men feel stifled by the pressures and demands to secure a steady paycheck or provide for their families. My friend Tim, a sculptor and visual artist who has always worked a regular job to pay the bills, shared that throughout his years in church he had always been told that his art was inconsequential. The message sent to him was that art was a hobby and "real men support their families properly." Now in his early sixties, Tim regrets not pursuing more of his dreams earlier. As his faith continues to be renewed, he is finding ways to create again. Over time he's breaking out of the message that he's not allowed, as a Christian man, to be an artist.

4. "You're Not Doing Enough"

June shared how a few years ago she was mentoring a young woman stuck in the ravages of the sex trade, hosting a thirty-five-person "small group" each week, leading a weekly moms' group, working with kids on Sunday mornings, trying to corral a group of church people to mentor a fourteen-member refugee family, plus trying to manage a rental, be a mom to three toddlers and wife to her husband, all while dealing with a huge crisis in her extended family. She called it "complete insanity"—and I have a feeling a lot of us have felt this craziness too!

When June mentioned to her pastor's wife that her marriage was strained under the demands of that much ministry, she was encouraged to sign up for an upcoming six-week marriage workshop. It was a dear friend outside the church system who told June the truth about the real issue: needing to slow down. Now, after a slow and laborious faith shift, she is working on becoming "a more thoughtful justice person rather than an urgent, breakneck activist." She is pursuing a master's degree in nonprofit management at a secular university. Her pace has changed radically. June is feeling stronger about these changes but admits those voices from the past rise up now and then, telling her she's not doing enough.

Because many of us have been faithful church or ministry volunteers for many years, we're hesitant to commit to too much because we know how quickly we can become overextended. It's good to be sensitive about this. As part of our Shifting process, we need a time of rest and disconnection from serving and giving. Yet, at some point, we have to face our fears and come out of hibernation. We have to try again even though it's scary. This time, though, we can pace ourselves and listen more intently to our souls and bodies along the way.

NEW SPIRIT, NEW PASSIONS

Sometimes when I talk to groups of men and women about pursuing their dreams, I can actually feel people begin to shut down. They are extremely wary of believing that dreams are possible. Thoughts of pursuing passions beyond stable employment seem too much. Often the unraveled are too jaded to dream.

But some of the core parts of Rebuilding our faith should be imagination and passion. If we stay stuck in fear, we will miss out on so much life. Our passions don't have to be big dreams like starting a nonprofit, becoming a high-profile leader, or going to college to get a different degree—although they might be. They can also be small steps toward doing what we love to do, such as figuring out what it even means to have a personal passion.

Often it is difficult to clearly hear from God the way we used to.

And honestly, maybe we are not even sure what "hearing God" means now. Regardless of whether we have an intense spiritual experience or a profound moment, we can listen to the quiet (or maybe loud) stirring in our hearts. Many of our passions center on three major areas—*love*, *justice*, and *beauty*. For those of you who may feel hesitant, unworthy, or unclear about how to start, here are a few major categories to consider:

A Passion to Love Practically

Passions in the love realm include loving people, being present, caring, serving, being Christ's hands and feet, reflecting God's image in hard places, and restoring dignity. There are countless ways to do this. Edward left church to hang out with homeless people, without any agenda. James started volunteering regularly at a local nonprofit, and Miranda decided to spend more time with some family members who desperately needed extra love and care during a difficult season. Samantha went back to school to become a children's grief therapist, and Marco started a ministry completely separate from the church he had attended. Jamie organized a coat drive at her kids' school, while Susanna started carrying around curb kits (snacks and personal care items) to pass out to people on street corners so her kids could participate too. Each of these activities flowed from a passion to love people in practical ways. In Rebuilding, we find we have more time and freedom to connect with people or needs in specific ways.

A Passion to See Justice Done

Justice is about creating structures and ministries that honor the dignity and worth of every human being. Many of us are advocates for causes. We want to stand on behalf of the oppressed and make what's wrong right by changing some of the existing systems. Some Rebuilders have become advocates for organizations that do direct justice work, such as rescuing children from human trafficking or serving people on the streets. Others became passionate about raising awareness about justice issues around the world through writing, speaking, or adopting children from foster care or Third World countries. Some started new ministries within their local churches, and others found simple but profound ways to live more justice-infused lives in their neighborhoods and daily lives. Grace, who is raising three young children after a messy divorce and running a thriving nonprofit, left traditional church but is finding new life as a vocal advocate for abused people—especially women—victimized by sex trafficking. Inside the church, she repeatedly hit walls as an outspoken female leader. Outside these confines, she is blossoming and her heart—and faith—is being renewed through her tangible justice work not only locally but globally as well.

A Passion to See and Create Beauty

Many Rebuilders care about nature, creativity, and the arts. They believe in the power of beauty to restore, inspire, and reveal God's image in people. After feeling dead and lifeless post-Unraveling, Lissa enrolled in a pottery class. It was a big step because she didn't feel creative or talented enough to ever make anything of it. Yet, as she started to feel the clay in her hands, sparks ignited in her heart and she discovered her new passion. Over the years her pots—just like her faith—have transformed from lopsided mugs to gorgeous vases. Through creating beauty, Lissa has discovered a deeper spirituality and has slowly come back to life.

Andrew calls himself an agnostic after a radical faith shift, but his heart is more alive than ever as he creates videos for small businesses trying to share their mission through storytelling. In small but powerful ways, his art has helped his heart come back to life after many of his prior beliefs died.

Passions fall into categories other than love, justice, and beauty, but these are great places to start. As we ignite our passions, our tender faith strengthens. Some of us have already found ways to live out what we love. The flame has been lit and the fire's roaring. Others may feel too scared to step out without the support and encouragement of the systems they used to be part of (or maybe still are). And some are unsure yet—any kind of passion still feels buried pretty deep. Regardless of where we find ourselves, part of rebuilding faith is igniting our passions—ones lying underneath a lot of rubble or ones recently discovered.

As our dreams take shape, we begin to explore fresh forms of community, connection, and "church" that look vastly different from where we used to serve. Next we will look at exploring possibilities for structures and pathways to nurture our ongoing spiritual development.

Questions for Personal or Group Reflection

1. Finish these sentences:

I am so happy when I _____. Or, I love to _____.

I care deeply for/about _____.

I get energized about _____.

I have always wanted to try _____, but I didn't think it was an option for me because _____.

I am really drawn to serving or partnering with _____.

2. This chapter fleshed out four potential obstacles to igniting our passions: 1) negative messages about our passions being selfish or worldly; 2) a pervasive feeling of inadequacy; 3) gender bias that has caused us to feel stifled in our gifts; and 4) fear of guilt for not contributing enough. Do you identify with any of these? What are other obstacles for you?

3. We briefly explored three broad categories of passions: love, justice, and beauty. Which are you drawn to? Why? What other areas of passion interest you?

4. What drew you to Jesus in the first place? Try to remember what you liked, loved, or were passionate about initially that became convoluted over the years.

5. How did you finish this sentence in question 1: I am really drawn to serving or partnering with _____? Find one aspect of this answer you could try in this next season of your life. It's brave to write it down and say it out loud.

6. What is a small next step you can take toward this passion? It might be doing the second half of question 5 and telling someone, or maybe it's making a phone call to get more information, signing up for a class, or showing up to volunteer.

Practicing Resurrection

I'm not sure I need a "church service,"
but I know I need community.

—Helen

Karl and I recently facilitated a gathering for people undergoing a church split involving wayward pastors, financial messes, and a whole lot of people left holding the bag. The level of pain in the room was intense, and I was reminded yet again how much damage destructive leadership has done in the name of God. My heart breaks because I know what is ahead for these dear and faithful men and women as they process their shattered church dreams.

Much of what Karl and I were hearing in that room led back to one question: *Will we ever be able to find or trust a church or community again?*

The question has no easy answers. Our experiences are wildly diverse, and life on the other side of a faith shift will always include a certain degree of mistrust of authority or systems. That's not a bad thing. In fact, it can mean we are wiser and more discerning, less apt to blindly give ourselves over to a confining system again. At the same time, we need people and structures in our lives that help us continue to grow. *Community* can be a pain-inducing word for many faith shift-ers, but we still need it—whether it's spiritual or not.

Elisa, once firmly entrenched in all things church, shared how deeply she misses community. She hadn't missed a Sunday before her faith shift, but since an intense Unraveling she has attended church only on Christmas and Easter; even then, she visits just one particular church because the pastor is a friend she trusts. Even though she has a challenging job and a happy life with her family and close friends, she longs for more connection on a regular basis. Elisa is lonely sometimes, but she's just not ready to reenter church and isn't quite sure she ever will be again. Often, even the thought of risking, trusting, trying, engaging again in any organized context feels too overwhelming. But part of moving forward as we rebuild our faith is exploring possibilities for community and connection.

What can help in the Rebuilding process is widening the defini-tion of what community and connection could be. It might mean finding a traditional faith community again or a group on the fringes. Maybe it's becoming part of a nonprofit organization, service club, online network, or a neighborhood group. It could mean creating your own group, designing the kind of gathering you need and inviting others with similar desires. Or maybe it's discovering a sacred space for intentional spiritual practices that help our souls. We've got to create more expansive definitions of what *community* can be.

We've also got to remain true to what we are learning about God and ourselves through this formation process. We've come too far to give it up for the sake of any system. We have to learn how to hold on to our truest selves and figure out how to show up in new ways.

This probably will require experiments, small excursions into un-charted territory. The key to exploring possibilities as part of Rebuild-ing is to ease in instead of rush, but also sometimes push through triggers instead of backing off every time we feel pain. As you read this chapter on potential options for church and community again, listen to what parts resonate for you and honor what you are ready to consider.

REFRAMING CHURCH

Our definitions of *church* are distorted based on our experiences. If it means a structure, a system with hierarchy, or a place to sing some songs and listen to someone talk once a week, faith shifters will reject it. But what if church was much more than that? What if we could redefine its parameters?

I know it won't meet the criteria of many theologians, scholars, and pastors, but my working definition of *church* is simple: "people gathered together to live, learn, and practice loving God, others, and themselves."

My daughter Julia is totally finished with church when it comes to organized religion. Still, she is deeply dedicated to cultivating a small community of friends at her college. They gather regularly in creative ways and are learning to live, learn, and love together. She would never call it church, but to me that's what it is. Sure, services can be helpful to people and create an intentional space to connect with God, but a service alone is not church. You don't need a bulletin, a pastor, an offering plate, a fog machine, or a song to make it church.

To me, church is anywhere people are connecting eye to eye, heart to heart, sharing life, breaking bread, carrying each other's burdens, being known, making themselves vulnerable, praying light into darkness, empowering, encouraging, and calling out God's image in each other. Sometimes that happens at specific spiritual services, but often church happens one-on-one, in coffee shops, in hospitals, in support groups, in houses, in shelters, at parties, and in groups of twos, threes, and fours. This kind of church deserves more credit. These meetings are where sustained healing happens, where the great loneliness subsides, where we feel alive and purposeful, where we feel loved and heard, and where the holy and the human intersect.

A lot of us might be more open to church if we felt greater freedom to reframe it with new models. Kyle and his wife feel passionately about changing their language to adapt to their lives after a faith shift. They no longer "go to church" but are finding life literally "being the church." They've given up attending services and Bible studies for hosting neighborhood parties and hanging out with people on the street.

Zoe, a recent college graduate, is serving in a nonprofit ministry dedicated to people on the margins, and her daily interactions provide plenty of church for her. Zach and Corrine, with decades of sobriety underneath their belts, consider their local AA group church, while some other girlfriends I know do church by hanging out once a month to share their lives and gather hope. A small group of people attend our Wednesday House of Refuge where we eat together and someone facilitates an interesting spiritual conversation. That's as much church as they can tolerate at the moment. Other dear friends make time regularly to attend a centering prayer group or are part of an online network of men and women with similar passions and interests.

Barbara Brown Taylor is a former pastor who wrote the poignant *Leaving Church: A Memoir of Faith.* She says,

> Although I never found a church where I felt completely at
> home again, I made a new home in the world. I renewed my
> membership in the priesthood of all believers, who may not
> have as much power as we would like, but whose consolation

prize is the freedom to meet God after work, well away from
all centers of religious command, wherever God shows up.[1]

Church exists in all kinds of ordinary, unlikely places, leaving us
a lot of possibilities to explore.

SLOW IS PLENTY FAST ENOUGH

I've noticed faith shifters tend to swing from one extreme to another.
We are often either all in or all out. Our hearts are either fully engaged
or clearly closed. The reality is that human beings aren't the best at
living in the middle. Exploring possibilities is a good way to practice a
healthier balance.

Though many shifters are extremely repulsed by all things church,
they often can dive into a new endeavor after Unraveling with as much
eagerness as they had during Fusing. We pour our energy, not in going
to church, but into our work, sports teams, online groups, start-up
nonprofits, or countless other efforts. We rush in and give our whole
hearts again in an effort to feel connected to something, anything.

There's nothing inherently wrong with this. Often, it's part of finding our way. It can also be dangerous because we are so lonely and
desperate for connection and stability that we might dive in too fast, too
hard, into whatever's right in front of us. That's what happened with me
and the Refuge. It saved me on one level, but part of my ongoing healing has been to maintain a healthy distance so that I can keep processing my feelings about God. This is not an easy task when I like the work
so much. But if I'm careful, I won't be consumed the way I was before.

Not everyone is like this. Many Rebuilders are far more tentative
and cautious. But if you are an all-in kind of person, you know what
I'm talking about. We can replace our addiction to church with an

addiction to other causes too. The words of Carl Jung ring true: "Every form of addiction is bad, no matter whether the narcotic be alcohol or morphine or idealism."[2]

On the other extreme, many people are completely shut down about anything churchy. But when we're trying to come back to life, we will have to engage with people and our faith somehow, or we'll never get to a new place. There's no way around it. We will have to make ourselves vulnerable.

In an effort to protect her heart after getting used up and burned out at her last church, June has hesitated to join in anywhere. A trigger for her is the phrase *get plugged in* (do you have a strong reaction to it too?). In the past, that concept has been a trick to lure people to serve the church's agenda. The dominant voice in her head says that stepping into any community or connection is all or nothing. But now, as June is slowly Rebuilding, she feels a gentle tug to risk her heart and move away from "nothing" but to stay away from "all."

SECRETS OF REENTRY

I encourage you, like June, to take your time on the fringes of whatever's next. Don't volunteer for too much too soon. Trust that healthy systems, groups, and people won't hurry you to engage when you're not ready. Recently a new couple moved to Denver after a messy church experience. They connected with the Refuge and have remained happily on the fringes, engaging slowly and taking care of their tender hearts. Recently they said they are ready to explore leading a new recovery group. I admit, I was drooling over the possibility of their leading something with us but didn't say anything. We laughed together recently about how while I was trying to be very careful about their feelings, they felt kind of bad I hadn't asked yet. At the same time, it was a healthy relief to them. The last thing they needed was to feel as if their only value was in leading.

Hold on to your personal power. Problems with systemic power are catalysts for many faith shifts. You will hurt your soul if you reenter a system with unbalanced power and inequality. I've observed that many women leave their current groups during a faith shift and then wrestle with the fact that they stayed in systems where leadership didn't value them properly. Yet after Shifting, they often find so few options of equality-infused community that they once again sacrifice their power. They attach to churches that might look a little kinder but still perpetuate the same subtle grooves of patriarchy and inequality.

Most of us need to be cautious about giving our power away to systems again. If you reengage and see warning signs, heed them. If you see leadership structures that cause you to feel squeamish, run for the hills. If you start to enter a group and discover gender inequality that concerns you, listen to your heart. You can find communities with healthy, balanced power structures. You may just need to give yourself time.

Of course, every system or group is going to be annoying in some way, and we have to give them a chance. Because of your sensitivity, be careful about prejudging people and communities. Part of exploring possibilities includes being gentle not only with ourselves but with others too. This means offering grace to leaders or other people who may use language that triggers painful memories or makes us feel uncomfortable. As we rebuild, we won't be able to create completely hypoallergenic environments and will constantly be faced with opportunities to develop greater resilience.

Embracing the idea of practice can be extremely helpful too. We can't expect to reengage with community one day and feel awesome and free the next. It takes practice to become more comfortable. Many once-evangelical faith shifters are drawn toward more liturgical churches. The radical difference in worship styles seems to allow re-builders to explore connection with God and others in a way that is life giving.

Lydia embodied the essence of an evangelical pastor's wife for many years. She sang the songs and played the part, but her soul was slowly dying inside. After a church split, she decided to try a deeply liturgical but socially progressive mainline denominational church. Lydia took a long time to adjust to the format, but she kept showing up and practicing. Slowly, surely, she found a new home for her heart and a community to hang out with, at least for now. She hasn't signed in blood to be a member forever; she's just a participant in a way that satisfies her soul and doesn't damage her heart.

Some other friends joined an online community for people strug-gling with their faith. For now, they are practicing sharing their stories and being challenged in that arena. They don't know each other out-side the Internet, but their hearts are connected online, and their expe-rience together is helping them heal, grow, and find their way. Will they be there forever? Probably not. But for now, it's a perfect place to practice being with other people who feel as they do.

Stephen has left traditional church, but as part of Rebuilding he decided to visit a small, missions-focused community in his town and see how they were serving the poor and marginalized. It meets in a coffee shop on Sunday mornings, and Stephen goes once in a while. He'd rather be out on the streets with people than sitting in a coffee shop, but he appreciates being with a few other people who care about the same things, and he feels challenged in interesting ways.

WIGGLY, SQUIGGLY LINES

All of these people are practicing. They are making themselves vulnerable instead of protecting their hearts forever. They are learning through new experiences and testing them against the important lessons they've gathered through Unraveling. They aren't locked into anything and can engage in a way that works for their souls.

If we try new experiences and they don't work, we don't have to let our disappointment ruin us. We can decide it's not for us. We can disagree with some things people in leadership say but be okay with others. We can remain skeptical about leadership and power but still take part. This doesn't make us cynical or uncommitted. It makes us wise.

Remember those wiggly, squiggly lines from Rebuilding in the faith evolution diagram we've been drawing? That's an important reality as we walk through these unpredictable steps of Rebuilding our faith. We will have to adjust along the way. We might take three steps forward and two steps back. It might hurt. It might feel awkward. That's okay. Rebuilding is about practice.

We have one last element to process before we end *Faith Shift*: keep trusting the path we are on and bravely continue to participate in ongoing resurrection as part of Rebuilding. It makes me think of the last stanza of the famous Wendell Berry poem, "Manifesto: The Mad Farmer Liberation Front":

Be like the fox
who makes more tracks than necessary,
some in the wrong direction.
Practice resurrection.[3]

Questions for Personal or Group Reflection

1. How would you draw or describe Rebuilding? What words or images come to mind?

2. How would you answer the question at the beginning of this chapter: Will I ever be able to find or trust a church or community again?

3. On a scale of 1 to 10 (with 1 being easy and 10 being hard), how do you feel about reengaging in some kind of church or community during this season of your journey?

4. What do you think of this definition of *church:* "People gathered together to live, learn, and practice loving God, others, and ourselves." What's your definition?

5. What are some forms of church or community you might be open to exploring? Remember, it doesn't have to be something overtly spiritual.

6. Do you dive in too deeply, too quickly, or stay on the edges, extremely hesitant about engaging? How could you step out of your comfort zone, just a bit, in this area? (For some it means slowing down, while for others it might mean trying when you don't feel like it.)

7. Considering the possibilities highlighted in this chapter, finish these sentences:

   I'd really like to try _____.

   I think I might like to experiment with _____.

   I am open to the possibility of _____.

Trust the Path Ahead

*After a while, you learn to ride the shifting
landscape like a surfer in the ocean. It
becomes thrilling rather than terrifying.
Then you can start to enjoy the ride.*

—DJ

The path for spiritual refugees like us rarely leads back to where we were. Usually it takes us around the next corner, and the next, further and further into the unknown, into diversity, mystery, and freedom.

Sophia, one of the wisest and most sincere faith shifters I have ever met, describes this kind of hard-won emancipation well:

I'm free from the fear that God is mad at me, free from the obligations of church leadership, free from the bubble of traditional Christianity's doctrinal limitations, free to think for myself and explore ideas I thought might be out of bounds before, free to explore the essence of my spirituality in ways that have nothing to do with ideology, free to support my gay friends, free from having to defend and understand God and God's ways.

The chains that used to bind Sophia have slowly slipped to the ground, and it's incredible to witness.

Freedom and new growth do not come cheaply or easily, but they are worth it. We have lost a lot in this process—people have ditched us; churches have dismissed us; leaders, friends, and family members have questioned us. We've doubted ourselves and wondered if we were just being rebellious. When I look back on the past years, I feel as though I was a soldier in a war. I'm coming out of it alive but with countless scars and battle stories. Through the process of writing this material I have been reminded how far I've come, and how freaky it feels not to know exactly where I'm going next.

In Rebuilding, water springs up where once was only desert. We begin to look forward instead of back. Hope rises. St. Augustine said, "Hope has two beautiful daughters. Their names are anger and courage: anger at the way things are, and courage to see that they do not remain the way they are."[1] Anger and courage are important companions for our transforming faith and provide the fuel we need to keep moving forward on this path.

Some people might have given up on us, but God hasn't. There is so much hope! A huge sign of life is that we are actually still in, trying to talk about this hard stuff and willing to engage with difficult questions and painful realities. People may criticize us and call us lost, angry, or a host of other adjectives, but the most enduring thing is that we're still trying to find our way toward God. That you are even bothering to read this book is a sign your faith is most definitely *not* dead. It's glorious that you are wrestling with cultivating a freer faith despite the costs.

Trust the path ahead, even though you aren't sure exactly where it will take you. You're not lost. In fact, you're on a road toward a bigger, better relationship with God, others, and yourself that will continue to develop.

The world doesn't need more fear-filled, insecure Jesus followers.

It needs more peace-filled, secure ones. It doesn't need more people deciding who's in and who's out on earth and in eternity. It needs more men and women who are passionate about drawing everyone toward the love of God.

Throughout the years, I have seen over and over again how this path leads to new beginnings, not endings, if we just keep walking. Thank you for taking this brave journey with me. Remembering my personal story of Fusing, Shifting, Returning, Unraveling, and ongoing Rebuilding has helped renew my faith.

Because *Faith Shift* was always meant to be interactive and personal, I would love to see your faith evolution diagrams and reflections and hear your evolving stories at www.kathyescobar.com. They won't just encourage me but others who need to find their way forward when everything they believe is coming apart. They, too, desperately need to know they're not crazy and they're not alone.

As we come together, please consider completing the sentences of what we call A Faith Shifter's Prayer. (If you are processing this material in a group, it's a great way to wrap up your time together.)

A Shifter's Prayer

God, I used to think you were _____.

I used to be able to say to others, to myself _____.

When I read the Bible I used to feel _____.

Now I sometimes feel _____.

Oh, how I miss _____.

But God, I'm trying to lean in to the present, to experience you in new ways.

I see you in _____.

I feel you in _____.

I hear you in _____.

I smell you in _____.

I touch you when I touch _____.

Thank you for these gifts.

Despite all the things I don't know, I can still cling to this _____.

And for that I am also thankful.

God, please keep sustaining me in these shifts.

I do want more of you in my life.

Amen.

Courage, peace, and hope to you as you keep walking this bumpy, beautiful path and start coming back to life!

Faith Shifts and Your Family and Friends

It's a harsh reality that most of us don't unravel in perfect synchronization with the people in our lives. It's hard enough to lose so much, but it's even more painful and lonely when your partner and kids can't relate to what you are going through. There is no way to cover all of the nuances of these relational dynamics, but here are a few suggestions to consider.

WHAT ABOUT THE SPOUSE?

Ways Faith Shifters Can Help Their Non-Shifting Spouses

- **Affirm the relationship.** "My relationship with God is changing, but I'm still here." For so many faithful Christ followers, church and life are so tangled up. When one person shifts, the other wonders what's left.

- **Ask what would help your partner.** In the same way faith shifters need help from the people around them, the spouses who haven't unraveled could use a little extra love too. It's appropriate to ask "What would help you right now?" You might not feel comfortable with whatever it is, but your willingness to extend an open hand matters.

- **Figure out what you would be willing to do.** For some, sitting in church is still a possibility, and if that helps your spouse feel less alone, it could be worth it. For others, that is too compromising, but you might be willing to attend some

other kind of meeting or gathering. You might not be able to
serve in ministries you used to be part of, but maybe there's
another place outside of church that feels possible. These
things can shift as time progresses, but they are small ways
to build security during an unstable time.

■ **Decide what is off the table for certain conversations.**
Some topics are simply too painful to discuss right now.
Talk through what these sensitive topics are and make some
decisions together about what living in the tension of this
transition can look like. This could mean not engaging in
some of these conversations in front of other people or when
you're too tired, scared, or angry. Counseling can sometimes be helpful as a safe place for having hard conversations and learning to better understand each other during
this season.

Ways Non-Shifting Spouses Can Help Faith Shifters

■ **Let go of control.** This is incredibly hard to do when you feel
so much is at stake! But your grip will in fact cause more angst
and pain for your spouse. It's good to meditate on the Serenity
Prayer: "God, grant me the serenity to accept the things I
cannot change, courage to change the things I can, and the
wisdom to know the difference." Trusting your partner's
process (even when to you it is confusing) is smart.

■ **Be a good listener.** Sometimes we think only about making
statements and saying what is on our hearts instead of listening to what our partners are wrestling with. We interject, we
explain, we state our positions. Good reflective listening means
checking for understanding without judgment: "So what I
hear you saying is…"

- **Practice validation.** Even when you do not hold the same viewpoint, it is valuable to say, "I see you, I hear you, and it makes sense why you might feel like that."

- **Hold your own truth.** It's important to own your own beliefs and not feel as if you need to give up your integrity in order to align with your spouse. It's also okay to say "It's lonely" and "I'm sad" about what's happening and still enjoy what your partner doesn't.

- **Ask what might help.** It's okay to make requests like these: "It would help me so much if you could come to this event with me." "Would you be willing to come to church with me once a month?" "Can you not talk bad about God in front of the kids?" It's also okay if your spouse just can't do what you want him or her to do. Your vulnerability is valuable here.

- **Accept the change.** It's true, things may never be the same again, and that will be something to grieve. Radical acceptance, though, is different from resignation. A new story is unfolding, and it can be a really beautiful one. Resistance over time will lead to anger and disconnectedness. Acceptance will lead to freedom and possibility.

WHAT ABOUT THE KIDS?

It's one thing for us to make a radical shift in how we live out our faith, but what does that mean for our children? They need stability and security, not questions and doubt. As a mom of five children, I am extra sensitive to the realities of a faith shift on the kids. We did the best we could, but there's no question, we made a lot of mistakes along the way. Each family's experience is different, and you will have to find what works for you, but I hope these ideas will help.

Ways Faith-Shifting Parents Can Help Their Kids

- **Kids don't need to know all the details.** We said too much
  out loud at a time when our oldest two kids were almost
  teenagers in Christian school. While some things can't be
  avoided when you live in the same house, my weeping, my
  anger about the church, and the specifics of how I had been
  hurt were details my kids didn't need to know. Frankly, it left
  them really confused. There's a way to be honest and authentic
  without exposing them to all the intricacies and emotions. I
  wish I had just said the truth: "I am going through a really
  weird season in my faith where I am struggling with God and
  the church, but I am going to be okay. We're going to be
  okay." I understand that you might be thinking, *I'm not sure I
  am going to be okay and I don't want to lie.* But I'll remind you:
  somehow, some way, you'll make it to a new place even
  though you're not sure what that place may be yet. Kids need
  this kind of security from their parents.

- **Kids can live without church programming.** It's okay to
  give that up. There are all kinds of ways to teach kids about
  God and faith without going to church on Sunday mornings. It's amazing how much instruction we have handed
  over to the church instead of engaging with it ourselves, and
  it's a good challenge not to rely on outside forces to teach
  our kids.

- **Kids can live with church programming.** It's okay to keep
  participating in church if that's what you choose. Faith
  shifters need to be cautious about what kids are being taught,
  but remember, kids love stories and ideas. There's a way to
  take part without having the church system infiltrate every

part of your family's lives and hearts. At the same time, it's important to stay on top of what they are being taught and not assume it's completely safe or doesn't matter. Ask questions and find out what they're learning. It's okay to disagree with teachings and talk about it together (depending on their age). I have said to my kids, "I don't agree with that" or "I don't interpret the Bible the same way they do," and it has helped them see that there are multiple perspectives. We need to be careful, though, that we are not part of systems where we are constantly at odds with teaching because that is too confusing for children.

■ **Focus on what you do still know.** My three youngest boys are probably the healthiest when it comes to spiritual things because they have been part of a free system for the longest. Even though there's a lot I doubt now, a few truths remain that I can pass on: God loves them, God will always be with them no matter what, and Jesus's ways are worth following. These truths have helped them become more secure.

■ **Discover what's going on with the kids by asking questions.** "What do you guys think about this?" became one of my favorite questions, because they always share the most amazing little kernels of beauty and truth. In my Fusing days I would have wanted to correct them and make sure they knew the "right" answers. Now, I appreciate their responses and acknowledge the richness of their thoughts even though they might be challenging. This means we, as parents, will have to live with answers that might freak us out or things they may say in front of our old friends from church. It's good to loosen our grip on these things, defuse power struggles, and let our kids participate in their faith development in a more organic way. We can teach our children to ask questions instead of blindly accepting whatever someone in authority is teaching them is "biblical."

- **Decide on your essentials.** Every family has its own essentials, but it's a good idea to decide and name what those might be. Then you know you can let go of the nonessentials and release guilt that you might carry for not passing on "enough" to the kids. Essentials are enough. Some of ours are *love God, love others, love yourselves in whatever ways you can.*

- **Trust their long-haul journeys.** It's easy to get caught up in the moment and see only our mistakes or what our kids are lacking. Every child has a life of spirituality ahead, and each will wrestle with faith in different ways over time. Seeing the big picture is wise. As you trust your own long-haul journey, you can trust theirs as well.

- **Actions are better than words.** Kids are visual learners. They love to practice, engage, and participate in learning. Instead of talking about our beliefs, we started acting on them by loving people, sacrificing our time for others, and just serving instead of talking about why we're supposed to do it. My husband went to law school a few years ago so he could get a second job serving domestic-violence victims as a pro bono lawyer. He didn't say "God wants us to do *x, y,* and *z* to serve him properly"—he just did it.

It's so hard to parent through a faith shift! It's scary, and my heart hurts for all of the suffering many parents have endured wondering if their choices were going to damage the kids. It's important to let go of perfectionism and control when it comes to this important task. We will mess things up. We will make mistakes. We will feel afraid. But in the end, the best we can offer is modeling our own authentic faith.

Remember, we're always doing the best we can with what we've got. This is tough stuff, but your caring about it matters.

Be kind and gentle with yourself. We'll need grace and mercy to fill in the cracks.

HOW TO BE A GOOD FRIEND TO SOMEONE IN A FAITH SHIFT

Lastly, if you haven't gone through a faith shift, it's hard to know what to do or say to a friend or family member who is in the midst of one. If you read this book to better understand, you are on the right track! Also, here are some practical ways you can support them:

- **Listen without judging, fixing, sharing scriptures, or giving advice.** This is hard to do when people we love are wrestling with deep questions, but the best gift we can give is to listen well. Almost every faith shifter I know has expressed that unsolicited scriptures have not helped but a kind, compassionate ear definitely has.
- **Respect anger.** It's part of grief that needs to be expressed if your loved one is to get to the other side. While anger is often difficult to watch or hear, it usually doesn't last forever.
- **Affirm the relationship over beliefs.** Remember, many faith shifters fear losing important relationships when they're struggling with their beliefs. Remind your friend or family member that you love him, not his beliefs, that you respect his process, and that you will be with him through it.

- **Let go of any timetables or expectations.** Each person's journey is unique, and it's important not to use measures like "once she goes back to church" or "starts serving again."
- **Ask what might help.** You can ask "What do you need right now?" or "How can I be a good friend to you during this season?"

Other Resources for Faith Shifters

Here are some tools to consider as you find your way. I'd love to find out what resources you have found to be helpful, so feel free to pass them on to me!

I hope we can connect on my blog, www.kathyescobar.com, and that some of the material there will help as you keep Rebuilding and finding hope and freedom.

Online Networks

The Lasting Supper (www.thelastingsupper.com). Facilitated by former pastor David Hayward, this group is a great place to process honest, raw feelings about a shifting faith.

Churchburned (www.churchburned.com). Facilitated by former pastor Travis Klassen, this online resource has articles and information centered on people hurt by the church.

Christians Tired of Being Misrepresented (www.christians tiredofbeingmisrepresented.blogspot.com). Articles and resources for people leaving fundamentalism but holding on to Jesus. This group also has an active Facebook group with over 77,000 followers.

Books

The Critical Journey: Stages in the Life of Faith by Janet Hagberg and Robert Guelich (Sheffield Publishing, 2004). I can't say enough how much I love this little book!

Evolving in Monkey Town: How a Girl Who Knew All the Answers Learned to Ask the Questions by Rachel Held Evans (Zondervan, 2010). This was rereleased in 2014 under a new title: *Faith Unraveled: How a Girl Who Knew All the Answers Learned to Ask Questions.* This is her memoir related to her own faith shift.

The Naked Now: Learning to See as the Mystics See by Richard Rohr (Crossroad Publishing Company, 2009). Anything by Richard Rohr is great, but this has some extra-good gems in it.

Leaving Church: A Memoir of Faith by Barbara Brown Taylor (HarperOne, 2007). A former minister, Brown relates her journey out of church in a beautiful book.

A New Kind of Christianity: 10 Questions That Are Transforming the Faith by Brian McLaren (HarperOne, 2011). Brian McLaren has been stirring the pot on Christianity for many years, and these questions are ones a lot of faith shifters are asking.

How to Be a Christian Without Going to Church: The Unofficial Guide to Alternative Christian Community by Kelly Bean (Baker, 2014). Kelly Bean has done an excellent job providing tangible possibilities for community outside traditional church.

The Inner Voice of Love by Henri Nouwen (Random House, 1998). All of Nouwen's books are soul stirring, but this one is especially appropriate for faith shifters. These are his private writings related to a personal crisis of faith and life.

Wide Open Spaces: Beyond Paint-By-Number Christianity by Jim Palmer (Thomas Nelson, 2007). Jim Palmer understands faith shifting and has some great material on his blog too at www.jimpalmerblog.com.

*Fundamorphosis: How I Left Fundamentalism But Didn't Lose
My Faith* by Robb Ryerse (Civitas Press, 2012). This is an
honest and raw story about Robb's shifting faith that those
leaving ultraconservative churches will really connect with.

Come Be My Light by Mother Teresa (Doubleday Religion, 2007).
Her private writings will help faith shifters find good company.

*The Ragamuffin Gospel: Good News for the Bedraggled, Beat-Up
and Burnt Out* by Brennan Manning (Multnomah Books,
2005). A classic that helps us remember that when we're on
the margins, we're in good company.

*When the Heart Waits: Spiritual Direction for Life's Sacred
Questions* by Sue Monk Kidd (HarperOne, 2006). She gives
raw and beautiful language to the realities of a spiritual
crisis and how to live in the in-between.

*The Dance of the Dissident Daughter: A Woman's Journey from
Christian Tradition to the Sacred Feminine* by Sue Monk
Kidd (HarperOne, 2006). A challenging read that helps
break open our limiting boxes about God and femininity.

*Love Wins: A Book About Heaven, Hell, and the Fate of Every
Person Who Ever Lived* by Rob Bell (HarperOne, 2012).
This book gives language to what a lot of faith shifters
begin to wonder about heaven and hell.

*A Generous Orthodoxy: Why I Am a Missional, Evangelical, Post
Protestant, Liberal/Conservative, Mystical/Poet, Charismatic/
Contemplative, Fundamentalist/Calvinist, Anabaptist/
Anglican, Methodist, Catholic, Green, Incarnational, De-
pressed but Hopeful, Emergent, Unfinished Christian* by Brian
McLaren (Zondervan, 2006). I included the subtitle
because it hits the nail on the head. As our faith shifts, we
open ourselves up to a much wider, more inclusive faith.

Torn: Rescuing the Gospels from the Gay-vs.-Christians Debate by Justin Lee (Jericho Books, 2013). Inclusive views on homosexuality are huge catalysts for faith shifts.

Christianity After Religion: The End of Church and the Beginning of a New Spiritual Awakening by Diana Butler Bass (HarperOne, 2013). Butler Bass helps us understand the wider shifts in Christianity through an honest lens.

Insurrection: To Believe Is Human, To Doubt, Divine by Peter Rollins (Howard Books, 2011). Rollins helps us understand how doubt is not only a natural part of faith but, indeed, divine.

Falling Upward: A Spirituality for the Two Halves of Life by Richard Rohr (Jossey-Bass, 2011). Almost any Rohr book is helpful for faith shifters, but this title is especially helpful in respecting that Unraveling is a natural part of simplifying our faith as we mature.

Down We Go: Living into the Wild Ways of Jesus by Kathy Escobar (Civitas Press, 2011). This book tells the story of the Refuge and fleshes out eight core practices of a downwardly mobile life that many faith shifters long to live out in some shape or form.

An Altar in the World: A Geography of Faith by Barbara Brown Taylor (HarperOne, 2010). Anything by Barbara Brown Taylor is worth reading, and this particular book challenges us to notice the sacred in the ordinary.

Traveling Mercies: Some Thoughts on Faith by Anne Lamott (Anchor Books, 2000). This oldie but goodie is a balm for the soul when it comes to a shifting faith. Lamott tells stories that widen our view of God in brilliant, beautiful ways.

Spiritual Formation: Following the Movements of the Spirit by Henri Nouwen (HarperCollins, 2006). A combination of Nouwen's writings and teachings over the years, the movements of this book are centered on the shift from the things that "are enslaving and destructive to something liberating and life giving." This book is good for Rebuilding, when we are opening ourselves up to new and old spiritual practices.

Daring Greatly: How the Courage to Be Vulnerable Transforms The Way We Live, Love, Parent, and Lead by Brené Brown (Gotham, 2012). While this material is not directly related to faith shifts, it is extremely helpful as we bravely move to new places in our lives. Her starting place is honesty and vulnerability.

Spiritual Direction

Finding a good spiritual director as a companion for your faith shift is so wise! Spiritual directors are different from therapists in that they focus on your journey with God in a very intentional and contemplative way. You can check out local resources at many Catholic or Episcopalian churches or connect with Spiritual Directors International at www.sdiworld.org to find an inclusive list of spiritual directors in your local area.

Also, sometimes a little therapy with a good professional counselor is a helpful place to start to clear out some of the initial emotions, and then move to spiritual direction over the long haul.

Acknowledgments

In the same way I never set out to be a pastor, I definitely never set out to be a writer! I started my blog in 2008 as a way to openly express some of the crazy stuff swirling around in my head related to faith, church, and life. I knew I needed to practice showing up, telling my truth, and living with disapproval publicly. It was one of the best decisions I ever made and opened the door to many incredible friendships that helped me find healing, hope, and courage in my shifting faith.

Faith Shift would not be possible without the encouragement, honesty, and incredible stories of my faithful blog readers and fellow faith shifters. You have helped me feel far less crazy and far less alone! Your response to the Rebuilding after Deconstructing series in 2012 was the genesis of this material and helped me realize how few tools exist to help us move forward when everything we believe is coming apart. When you commented, sent e-mails, posted on Facebook and Twitter, or whispered to me in passing that you read my blog that day and it was healing, you kept me going.

I'd also like to offer my deep gratitude to the Refuge community, which has truly been my safe space for the past eight years. Your courage, vulnerability, and friendship have inspired me to stay the course and navigate my changing faith with more integrity than I ever could have on my own. I'm grateful to be in a place where these kinds of conversations aren't taboo but welcomed. I especially want to thank Stacy Schaffer, Sage Harmos, Megan Harris, and Phyllis Mathis for their editing, love, and input in the early stages of this book. They were with me on *Down We Go,* too, and the time and tenderness they freely gave to this project was an incredible gift to me.

I will always be thankful to David Kopp and Susan Tjaden, editors from Convergent Books, who contacted me about writing for them and then helped form this project with me. I knew from the beginning this was what I needed to write, and they helped me pull it all together from start to finish. With the addition of Holly Halverson to the editing team, there were a lot of cooks in the kitchen! But I have to say that, in the end, I think we made a pretty decent meal together.

Last, none of what I do is possible without my amazing husband, Jose, who is the best juggler, cheerleader, and teammate ever. With five kids, crazy schedules, and the realities of this life we have chosen, I often wonder how we get anything done. Somehow we have managed to do this all together, but it's only because he cooks, cleans, holds down the fort, and best of all, makes me laugh every single day.

Notes

Chapter 1

1. Matthew Green, *"Why are So Many Christians Quitting Church?"* *Charisma Magazine (blog)*, December 12, 2012, http://www .charismamag.com/spirit/church-ministry/7279-the-church -dropout/.

2. Barna Group, https://www.barna.org/teens-next-gen-articles/ 528-six-reasons-young-christians-leave-church.

3. Joseph Sirba, http://www.hprweb.com/2009/01/the-u-s-religious -landscape-survey/, "The U.S. Religious Landscape Survey," *Homiletic and Pastoral Review* (blog), January 1, 2009, http:// www.hprweb.com/2009/01/the-u-s-religious-landscape-survey/; "Rise of the Nones," *Time Magazine,* vol. 179, no. 10: 68, quoted in Randy Newman, "The Rise of the 'Nones,'"www.randy davidnewman.com (blog), April 5, 2012, http://www.randy davidnewman.com/2012/04/05/the-rise-of-the-nones/.

4. Janet Hagberg, and Robert Guelich, *The Critical Journey: Stages in the Life of Faith* (Salem, OR: Sheffield Publishers, 2005); James Fowler, *Stages of Faith: The Psychology of Human Development and the Quest for Meaning* (San Francisco, CA: Harper Collins, 1981).

   The Hagberg/Guelich material was extremely transforming for me and gave language to my experience. Their focus on "hitting the Wall" and taking a "journey inward" will resonate with so many faith shifters. Fowler's is the most prominent academic work on the stages of faith and has also been helpful to many.

Chapter 2

1. Richard Rohr's Daily Meditations, "Emotional Freedom and Ecumenism," July 10, 2013, http://myemail.constantcontact .com/Richard-Rohr-s-Daily-Meditations--Emotional-Freedom ----Ecumenism----July-10--2013.html?soid=1103098668616&ai d=xbdCRwhhSoE.

Chapter 3

1. Henri Nouwen, *Making All Things New: An Invitation to the Spiritual Life* (New York: Harper Collins, 1981), 55.

Chapter 4

1. Barna Group, "Six Reasons Young Christians Leave the Church," September 28, 2011, https://www.barna.org /teens-next-gen-articles/528-six-reasons-young-christians -leave-church.
2. Rachel Held Evans, "How Evangelicals Won a Culture War and Lost a Generation," *CNN Belief Blog* (blog), March 31, 2014, http://religion.blogs.cnn.com/2014/03 /31/how-evangelicals-won-a-culture-war-and-lost-a -generation/.
3. David Kinnaman, "You Lost Me: Young Christians Rethink Faith," *Faith Matters,* http://www.npr.org/2012/01/20 /145518098/you-lost-me-young-christians-rethink-faith.
4. Mother Teresa, *Come Be My Light* (New York: Doubleday Religion, 2007), 187.
5. Hemant Mehta, "Why are Christians Leaving the Church? It Turns Out It's the Churches' Fault," *Friendly Atheist* (blog), September 29, 2011.

Chapter 5

1. Henri Nouwen, *The Inner Voice of Love: A Journey of Anguish to Freedom* (New York: Random House, 1998), 21.

Chapter 6

1. Brené Brown, *Daring Greatly: How the Courage to Be Vulnerable Transforms The Way We Live, Love, Parent, and Lead* (New York: Penguin Group, 2012), 34.
2. Brené Brown, *The Gifts of Imperfection* (Center City, MN: Hazelden, 2010), 41, emphasis in original.

Chapter 7

1. Hope Edelman, *Motherless Daughters: The Legacy of Loss* (New York: Dell Publishing, 1994), 5.
2. C. S. Lewis, *A Grief Observed* (New York: Harper Collins, 1961), 15.
3. Rumi, *The Essential Rumi,* trans. Coleman Barks with John Moyne (New York: Harper Collins, 1995), 54.

Chapter 8

1. Henri Nouwen, *Finding My Way Home: Pathways to Life and the Spirit* (New York: Crossroads Publishing, 2001), 137.
2. Sue Monk Kidd, *The Dance of the Dissident Daughter* (New York: Harper Collins, 1996), 34.
3. Rachel Held Evans, *Evolving in Monkey Town* (Grand Rapids, MI: Zondervan, 2010), 17–18.
4. Phyllis Tickle, *The Great Emergence* (Grand Rapids, MI: Baker Books, 2008).

Chapter 9

1. Anne Lamott, *Help, Thanks, Wow: The Three Essential Prayers* (New York: Penguin Books, 2012), 37.

2. Diana Butler Bass, *Christianity After Religion* (New York: Harper Collins, 2012), 69.

3. Peter Rollins, "Dawkins, Dennett and Hitchens: The New Theists?" *Peter Rollins* (blog), October 3, 2013, http://peter rollins.net/2013/03/dawkins-dennett-and-hitchens-the-new -theists/.

Chapter 10

1. Dan Allender, *The Wounded Heart: Hope for Adult Victims of Childhood Sexual Abuse* (Colorado Springs, CO: NavPress, 1990), 54.

2. Melody Beattie, *Codependent No More* (Center City, MN: Hazelden, 1986), 147.

3. Cheryl Lawrie, "Fitzroy" *Hold This Space* (blog), May 28, 2009, http://www.holdthisspace.org.au/fitzroy. Reprinted with permission.

4. Mary Karr, *Lit* (New York: HarperCollins, 2009), 260.

Chapter 11

1. Anne Lamott, *Plan B: Further Thoughts on Faith* (New York: Penguin Books, 2005), 295–96.

Chapter 12

1. Anne Lamott, *Traveling Mercies: Some Thoughts on Faith* (New York: Random House, 1999), 126.

2. Rhoda Janzen, *Mennonite in a Little Black Dress* (New York: Henry Holt and Company, 2009), 137.

3. Sara Miles, *Take This Bread* (New York: Ballantine Books, 2007), 161–62.

4. Gary Thomas, *Sacred Pathways* (Grand Rapids, MI: Zondervan, 1996).

5. Coleman Barks, *The Rumi Book of Love: Poems of Ecstasy and Longing* (New York: Harper Collins, 2003), 123.

Chapter 13

1. Alex Haley in Janet Cheatham Bell, *Famous Black Quotations* (New York: Warner Books, 1986), 125.

2. Barbara Brown Taylor, *An Altar in the World: A Geography of Faith* (New York: HarperOne, 2010), 117–18.

3. Richard Rohr, *The Naked Now: Learning to See as the Mystics See* (New York: Crossroad Publishing, 2009), 132.

4. Brennan Manning, *The Ragamuffin Gospel* (Sisters, OR: Multnomah Publishing, 2005), 23.

Chapter 14

1. St. Irenaeus, quoted in Philippe Delhaye, *Pope John Paul on the Contemporary Importance of St. Irenaeus, L'Osservatore Romano,* February 9, 1987, 6. *Ewtn.com* (blog), http://www.ewtn.com /library/theology/irenaeus.htm.

2. Eleanor Roosevelt, quoted in Gordon Livingston, *The Thing You Think You Cannot Do* (Philadelphia, PA: Da Capo Press, 2012), xxi.

3. Brown, *Daring Greatly,* 89.

Chapter 15

1. Barbara Brown Taylor, *Leaving Church: A Memoir of Faith* (New York: HarperCollins, 2006), 166.

2. Carl Jung, *Memories, Dreams, Reflections* (New York: Random House, 1989), 329.

3. Wendell Berry, *The Country of Marriage* (Berkeley, CA: Counterpoint, 2013), 15.

Chapter 16

1. Robert McAfee Brown, *Spirituality and Liberation* (Louisville, KY: Westminster Press, 1988), 136.

About the Author

A pastor, mom, wife, advocate, speaker, and spiritual director, Kathy Escobar's greatest love is journeying with people in hard places and seeing hope come from despair. She founded and co-pastors the Refuge (www.therefugeonline.org), a mission center and Christian community in North Denver and is passionate about creating healing communities for those on the margins of life and faith.

A California transplant to Colorado, she's happiest when near the water with her husband, Jose, and their five children. The Escobars can often be found at their local lake water-skiing and wakeboarding during the summer or traveling to a beach during Denver winters.

Kathy holds a BA in organizational communication from Pepperdine University, an MA in management from John F. Kennedy University, and a certificate in Evangelical Spiritual Guidance from Denver Seminary.

She has written several other books, including *Come with Me: An Invitation to Break Through the Walls Between You and God; Refresh: Sharing Stories, Building Faith;* and *Down We Go: Living into the Wild Ways of Jesus.* Kathy blogs regularly about life and faith at www.kathyescobar.com and always loves to hear from readers.

Connect with Kathy at
Website: http://www.kathyescobar.com
Twitter: @kathyescobar
Facebook: https://www.facebook.com/kathyescobarauthor